PACIFIC CREST TRIALS

Zach Davis and Carly Moree

ACKNOWLEDGMENTS

From Zach: Although my and Carly's names are the ones who grace the cover of this book, to say that we were the only two who poured energy into it's creation would be disingenuous.

First and foremost, I would like to again thank all those who played an instrumental role in the creation of *Appalachian Trials*, which serves as the foundation for this book. You know who you are.

Doug "Poppa Doc" Hankes, Ph.D, thank you for making good on a two-year-old offer to lend your expertise to this project. Dear reader, do yourself a favor and head to bit.ly/DonutPizza. The dirty hiker trash with the salt and pepper beard in the background is the director of the counseling center at Auburn University and formerly served as the sport psychologist for their athletic department. *The people you'll meet on the trail.*

Thank you to the countless PCT thru-hikers who were willing to let us pick your brain and share your story. A special shout out goes to Tee "Jambo" Corley, Kristin "Siren" McLane, and "Mac" for injecting your gift with words into this book.

Thank you Maggie Slepian for being my ever-reliable Swiss Army knife of an aide. Whatever task I throw your way, you handle with grace. You are a rock star.

Thank you to my loving girlfriend, Jenna, who had a front row seat for the roller coaster of emotions I exhibited while putting this together. A lesser human being would've shoved a pacifier in my mouth.

And once again, Mother Badger, thank you for the constant support and inspiration to follow in your giant, size-7 footsteps. Big goals feel attainable in large part because of your example.

From Carly: A huge thank you, spanning the distance of Mexico to Canada and then some, to the following people for making this a possibility!

Jolly, Siren, Snooze, Par 3, Jeffe, thank you for your contributions and feedback!

To the gents at *Simply*Home, thank you for your encouragement and facilitation to help me thru-hike the PCT...twice!

Kristina, you got me to the AT trailhead emotionally and then literally got me to the PCT trailhead. An impressive feat, for which I am forever grateful.

Holly, thanks for being a constant source of support and always reminding me to keep that *roar*.

Thank you Mamacita and Dad for always being accepting of whatever crazy ideas I throw your way and then taking this a step further in helping me to accomplish them.

Shades, Tutone, Chia, Sluggy, T-Sniffs, Boomboxxx, and Pogo, thank you for always making me laugh uncontrollably, both on and off trail. Club Q holds a special place in my heart.

Kristen, what can I say? You get it. "Here is the deepest secret nobody knows (here is the root of the root and the bud of the bud and the sky of the sky of a tree called life; which grows higher than soul can hope or mind can hide) and this is the wonder that's keeping the stars apart. I carry your heart (I carry it in my heart)."

Table of Contents

"You cannot stay on the summit forever; you have to come down again. So why bother in the first place? Just this: What is above knows what is below, but what is below does not know what is above. One climbs, one sees. One descends, one sees no longer, but one has seen. There is an art of conducting oneself in the lower regions by the memory of what one saw higher up. When one can no longer see, one can at least still know."

- René Daumal

- Introduction -

So, you want to thru-hike the Pacific Crest Trail? You're taking all the steps necessary to prepare yourself. You're leaving no stone unturned. You're reaching out to former thru-hikers. You've already memorized every page of Yogi's Pacific Crest Trail Handbook. You've spent more time reading PCT blogs than you can recall. You've lost sleep over whether you should bring a sleeping bag or quilt, tent or tarp, and which bear canister to buy. You've mapped out every location where mail drops will be sent.

And then somehow you stumbled upon this book.

"A psychological guide? To hiking? Let me guess, one foot in front of the other. Do this approximately 5.3 million times and you have successfully walked from Mexico to Canada. It's as simple as that, right?"

Right. Except for one thing, the five point three million part.

You might assume that the most difficult aspect of walking the Pacific Crest Trail's 2,650 mile distance would be purely physical. Undoubtedly, thru-hiking the Pacific Crest Trail is a daunting physical feat. You will push your body to new extremes. You will sweat. You will struggle. You will wake up and fall asleep sore. With that said, the physical challenge is not what causes countless numbers of aspiring thru-hikers to fall short of their goal.

In no uncertain terms, the psychological and emotional struggle is what drives people off the Pacific Crest Trail; those struggles are the basis of your very own Pacific Crest trials.

It's soul-crushing homesickness and loneliness. It's arid, sweltering, desert heat. It's dealing with consecutive days of maddening thirst while calculating the number of steps you can take between sips of water; rationing sucks. It's trying to sleep through sub-freezing temperatures above treeline, hoping that wearing every article of clothing in your pack and wrapping your sleeping bag over your head will provide enough warmth to grant a few hours of sleep. It's getting to town and learning that the next 80-miles of the trail are closed due to wildfires.

It's hiking through a swarm of mosquitoes. It's boredom that comes from three days worth of seemingly identical terrain. It's pain that strangleholds every muscle of your body upon waking. It's putting on the same sweat-soaked clothes for a consecutive week. It's pooping in the rain; have fun trying to wipe. It's your hiking partner informing you that he just purchased his flight home, less than one month into your thru-hike; now what?

It's drinking discolored stream water. It's getting hit with an unexpected snowstorm. It's wandering a mile off trail before realizing you have no idea where you are. It's living in a constant coat of sweat, sunscreen, and sand. It's simultaneously realizing that the only thing remaining in your food bag is a Clif Bar and mustard packet, with 21 miles to go before town. It's walking for days on end with a set of throbbing blisters between your toes and on the sides of your heels. It's arriving to a water cache that you were relying on, only to learn it's been entirely consumed.

It's veering off trail to go to the bathroom, only to look down and notice that you've just walked through Poodle-Dog Bush. It's running through a storm while lightning crashes down on all sides of you. It's an animal rustling outside your tent just moments before you were going to fall asleep.

These are the reasons people throw in the towel, not because a climb is too daunting.

That's why all the how-to advice in the world regarding logistics and terrain, while important, will do nothing to keep you inspired enough to stick with your goal when the going gets tough. Going through the hassle of devising an elaborate resupply schedule, a conventional pre-trail strategy, gives the illusion of essential preparation, but in reality, a solid percentage[1] of aspiring thru-hikers won't make it to all of their resupply locations. If a mail-drop is sent, but no one is there to receive it, does it really exist? Let's be clear, if finishing the Pacific Crest Trail is your goal, your time could be better spent.

Many successful thru-hikers have gotten by without sending a single mail drop before leaving for Campo. That's not to say this is the best strategy for *your* needs. The point is, focusing on your resupply strategy before honing in on your mental preparation is like sharpening your pencil as your primary means of preparing for a test.

So, who are we to insist that preparing your brain is the most important aspect of a thru-hike?

I am Zach Davis, the primary voice of this book. *Hey, how's it going?* I thru-hiked the Appalachian Trail in 2011. Prior to my departure, I had exactly zero backpacking experience. I learned how to pitch a tent just a few nights before leaving for the trail. Simply put, I was as incompetent about living outdoors and long-distance backpacking as it gets.

Beginning in the months leading up to my journey all the way through finishing my thru-hike, I kept a running diary on my blog: theGoodBadger.com. I wasn't interested in the day-to-day details of backpacking; the names of summits, gaps, and bodies of water go in one ear and out the other. Instead, what interested me were the mind games, trail culture, emotional rollercoaster, and personal metamorphosis that comes along with living outside for half a year. On my blog, I detailed not only my struggles, but the larger trends I noticed among my hiking peers. Before I knew it, I was getting more traffic and positive feedback to my website in a single month than I had in the previous year.

Apparently I struck a chord.

When I finished the trail, I wanted to find a book detailing the psychological aspects of thru-hiking to see

---

[1] The Pacific Crest Trail Association, the nonprofit that oversees the PCT, does not keep an accurate record of completion rate stats. Their website used to estimate somewhere near 50%.

how it compared to my experiences. What I found baffled me. This book didn't exist. There are a plethora of how-to books, none of which deal with the most challenging aspect of the trail?!

Fine, I'll do it.

In the months following the completion of my thru-hike, I wrote *Appalachian Trials: A Psychological and Emotional Guide to Successfully Thru-Hiking The Appalachian Trail*. Since you and I are now BFF, I'm going to let you in on a little secret: I didn't write *Appalachian Trials* with the expectation of selling tens of thousands of copies, eventually quitting my nine-to-five to run a website by the same name[2]. I wrote the book because it seemed like a reasonable excuse to not get a job, or at least delay the process. Once the book was published, I figured my family, friends, and a couple handfuls of the people who read my personal blog would buy a copy and that would be the end of it.

Thankfully, as it turned out, I was wrong. The book took on a life of its own and continues to serve as one of the top resources for aspiring AT thru-hikers today[3].

In the years that have passed since publishing *Appalachian Trials*, I've received countless messages from thru-hikers thanking me for writing the book; they tell me that it played a huge role in their success. Many have even told me the book was the difference maker. After completing her 2014 thru-hike, Amy "Stardust" Long wrote, "I wouldn't have finished my hike if I had not read *Appalachian Trials*."[4]

Now I can hear your skepticism, "Great, you hiked the AT. What does that have to do with the Pacific Crest Trail?"

It's a fair question that deserves addressing.

First and foremost, *Appalachian Trials'* message is as much about the Appalachian Trail as To Kill a Mockingbird

---

[2] Which is ultimately what happened.

[3] According to a survey conducted by the Appalachian Trail Conservancy, the nonprofit that oversees the AT, *Appalachian Trials* was named the most popular book amongst 2014 thru-hikers.

[4] From Amy Long, a 2014 AT thru-hiker. Check out wrote her inspirational, heart-warming post-thru-hike wrap up article: http://appalachiantrials.com/victory-mine/

is about killing birds. In reality, it's a self-help book disguised as a thru-hiking book[5]. Although the details are written specifically for those who are gearing up to hike the AT, the principles are broad and far-reaching.

Several of *Appalachian Trials'* Amazon reviewers agree. Here's but a small sampling:

"Absolutely a must for 'any' thru hike or even a long distance backpacking journey...I highly recommend this work. I've been backpacking for 40+ years even doing it with our Nation's best, most elite soldiers--the Army's Special Forces (Green Berets). Take it as gospel, this is very helpful even for daily life." - Michael King

"I very much wish I had read this book before my thru-hike in 2012, as I feel I would have saved myself a lot of unnecessary stress, worry, self-doubt, and other mental tail-chasing while on the trail...Highly recommend to any aspiring thru or section hiker, or pretty much anyone looking to improve their perspective and their life." - Brian Bisesi

"Whether it's a long distance thru-hike or joining the Peace Corps, you should read this book if you plan to willingly put yourself through something mentally, emotionally, and/or physically taxing." - Alexander

With that said, *Appalachian Trials* does tell this story through the lens of thru-hiking the Appalachian Trail. Similarly, Pacific Crest Trials tells this story through the lens of thru-hiking the Pacific Crest Trail. "How?" you ask.

Enter my co-author, Carly "Papi" Moree.

After hiking the AT in 2013, Carly successfully thru-hiked the Pacific Crest Trail in 2015. Like me, Carly's primary fascination with thru-hiking has less to do with the

---

[5] I purposely refrain from referring to it as a self-help book when possible as people tend to shy away from admitting they need help. This is a huge mistake. Everyone can benefit from seeking improvement. Those whose prides intervene are doing themselves a disservice.

day-to-day specifics and more about the people of the trail. We both enjoy long walks. We both enjoy a good beer. That's about where the similarities end. Carly is an extrovert who prefers hiking in groups. I am an introvert who needs a nap after talking to a new person for more than 15 minutes. Carly is vegan, I am a borderline-carnivore. Carly naturally goes with the flow, my programming is more set to "control freak". Carly is female, I have man parts.

It is due to all of these reasons (and more) that I sought Carly's assistance in taking on Pacific Crest Trials. In addition to her input on every word in this book, Carly's unique vantage point helped me see thru-hiking through a new lens. Additionally, over the course of writing this book, Carly and I interviewed *dozens* of other PCT thru-hikers to get an even more robust understanding of people's common struggles, coping mechanisms, and the trail's culture. It is my sincere belief that Pacific Crest Trials is a thorough resource that will help you accomplish your goal- thru-hiking the PCT.

One more thing: if you've already read *Appalachian Trials*, you do not need to buy this book. Many of the themes are the same. You're already equipped with the psychological tool-set necessary to take on the AT, PCT, and all the other T's. Get to hiking already.

The Goal

Over the course of your PCT journey, you will encounter three categories of people:

1. Those who succumb to the mental challenges and quit
2. Those who rely on sheer determination, grit their teeth, and press on to Canada, despite being at odds with the process
3. Those who enjoy most, if not all, of their experience while successfully thru-hiking the Pacific Crest Trail

This book will put you in the third category.

People who fall into the first group, in my opinion, fail themselves before they even leave home. They pour hours into researching their gear, digging through backpacking forums and blogs about the pros and cons of rain pants versus skirts. Then they begin planning every single one of their mail drops. They dump hundreds of dollars into Costco bulk purchases, dividing into proper macronutrient ratios, and meticulously tallying to ensure they're consuming at least 3,500 calories per day. Next comes the elaborate mail drop spreadsheet, with locations, hours, phone numbers, and distance between stops.

Lastly, it's the physical preparation. Five to ten hours at the gym each week builds a solid muscular frame and endurance base. Maybe a few shakedown hikes to hone in on what works and what doesn't and to get familiar with sleeping outside. And that's it; that's where the preparation ends. The most important factor of a thru-hike, the mental component, is totally neglected. With the first instance of true adversity, their white flag goes up, and it's over.

Months, if not years, of planning, all for naught.

While their level of determination is admirable, I don't want you to fall into this second group. These individuals struggle through the lion's share of their trek, relying on stubbornness to propel themselves to the finish. For the entirety of their hike, the focus is to get to Canada, with the destination taking precedence over the journey. It's important to keep in mind that the Pacific Crest Trail is a five-month unpaid vacation. How determined would you have to be to sit on a beach, sipping Mai Tais for the same time span? The trail should be enjoyed, and when joy is difficult to achieve, personal growth should become the focus.

Still, you might be skeptical. Perhaps you're thinking, "People who would love a half-year backpacking trip possess a rare and inherent quality; they're wired differently. It's built into their DNA, and I just wasn't bestowed with those attributes." I understand why you might feel this way, and quite frankly, some people do fit this mold. The overwhelming majority, however, do not. I genuinely enjoyed thru-hiking a 2,200 mile trail and I am the furthest thing from this description.

While growing up, my parents would force my sister and me to go on short hikes. Many say their love affair with the outdoors began in such a way. This was not the case for me. After about a quarter of a mile, I would show my disdain for such aimless walking with a sitting protest[6]. Oftentimes, the only way my parents could convince me to continue was by bribing me with peanut M&Ms. I was fat.

Even after developing a love for exercise in my late teens (bye, fat Zach!), my preference was indoor sports- running on a treadmill so I could watch TV, riding on a stationary bike so I could read a book, indoor basketball because the wind would force me to shoot airballs (apparently there's wind inside too). I had zero interest in being outdoors, and certainly not deep into the backcountry, far from my creature comforts.

Leading up to my departure, there was no one more ill-prepared to thru-hike than me. I was a computer guy, not a camping guy. I owned none of the gear necessary for a half-year backpacking trip. I had never set up a tent or built a campfire. The only thing I had going for me was that I was in decent shape and good health. But as you will learn in Chapter 6, even that was taken away from me. Now that I've completed this task, I look back at my experience with only fond memories, even when sober.

The bottom line is this: not only can you achieve your goal of hiking from Mexico to Canada[7], you can, and should, enjoy the process. This book will show you how.

Since you picked up this book, I feel responsible for your success. Your completing the PCT and enjoying the process sincerely matters to me. I'm convinced the rest of the book will help you accomplish just that.

But there is another reason you should read Pacific Crest Trials. You're not the only one who will be presented with psychological hurdles. Family and friends who are clueless about your upcoming adventure may be anxious as well. And trust me on this one, calming their fears benefits

---

[6] Unfortunately, there is proof of this. http://bit.ly/ZachIsFat

[7] This book is written with the perspective of a NOBO thru-hiker in mind. If you're in the minority who take on a SOBO thru-hike, simply flip this book upside down.

you. They'll get off your back. They'll join your team. They'll applaud your seemingly idiotic journey instead of questioning it, because, after all, knowledge assuages fear. So when you're done reading this book, pass it on to the anxiety-ridden people in your life. Better yet, tell them to get their own copy.

Here's another reason reading this book should be on your short list of things to do before leaving for the trail. Perhaps you're someone who isn't yet convinced traversing the country's first established national scenic trail is something you want to do[8]. The fact that you're reading this book tells me that you're sufficiently curious about it. With a little nudge, you might just decide to leave behind the comforts of home and embark on the journey of a lifetime. At the very least, you'll get a sneak peak into the psyche of a thru-hiker. Knowing what's in a thru-hiker's pack is nice. But if finishing is your concern, knowing what's inside a thru-hiker's mind is what matters.

I'm convinced that for every person who actually embarks on the PCT, there are countless others who talk themselves out of it for one reason or another. Don't be one of those people. Not only will I provide that friendly nudge to pack your pack, I'll be with you every step along the way.

This book is divided into four sections. The first three- pre-trail, on-trail, and (you guessed it) post-trail- will both prepare you against the common pitfalls aspiring thru-hikers fall into, as well as provide you the necessary tools to keep a strong mindset when you're confronted with your own Pacific Crest trials. The fourth section is a collection of bonus material including an incredible gear chapter from triple crowner Liz "Snorkel" Thomas and the necessity for adaptation during your thru-hike.

One final note- throughout *Pacific Crest Trials*, there is an emphasis on the challenges associated with thru-hiking the Pacific Crest Trail. Our objective with this book is to prepare you for the obstacles that you can expect to encounter during a half-year on the trail. The only way we can properly accomplish this is by shining a light on these

---

[8] Technically tied for first with the Appalachian Trail as it was established in 1968 under the National Trails System Act.

darker regions. We're going to tell it like it is, which is likely not how you've heard it from others. For this reason, however, it could be interpreted that we have a negative perspective of the PCT or thru-hiking. Nothing could be further from the truth. My thru-hike was the best five months and one day of my life to date. Carly enjoyed her PCT thru-hike so much that she's doing it all over again in 2016. Thru-hiking is life transforming in a positive way.

So whether you're already planning your journey into the wilderness or you're still straddling the fence, let's head over to Chapter 1, where you'll get a glimpse my pre-hike self, convincing you evermore that if I was able to thru-hike, you will too.

SECTION ONE:
PRE-TRAIL

CHAPTER 1 -
COMPUTER NERD
TURNED BEAR GRYLLS

I t was early November. I had mentally committed to the insane: next spring I would backpack from Georgia to Maine. It was almost too ridiculous to comprehend. In a state of excitement / bewilderment I called Mitch, a former roommate and good friend.

> **Me**: Guess what?
> **Mitch**: What?
> **Me**: I'm going to hike the Appalachian Trail...
> **Mitch**: (Without hesitation) Pshht. No you're not.
> **Me**: Wait....what? You don't even know what it is. How can you be so dismissive?
> **Mitch**: My sister's boyfriend is a former thru-hiker. They live in a town right on the trail. I know plenty about the AT, and there's no way you're going to hike the whole thing.

There are two takeaways from the above conversation.

1. Someone who knew me well put my chances of successfully completing a thru-hike at zero.
2. I need new friends.

At the time of this conversation, I had slept in a tent a total of two nights - once on a car camping trip, once in a friend's backyard. I set up a tent zero times, which matched my experience in building fires or fastening a fully-loaded backpack. My entire outdoor repertoire consisted of drinking beer near a campfire (which I'm quite good at), pretending I could accurately reproduce animal mating calls (I can't) and scorching marshmallows (I sorely lack patience).

A friend once said that if pressed to list "Zach's Skill Set for Survival in Nature", my "affinity for bandanas" would rank #1, which, as it turns out, is not even a skill.

In other words, although Mitch's response lacked tact, his assessment was fair.

So why would someone who had never been backpacking in his entire life want to take part in a cross-country backpacking trip?

In a word: dissatisfaction.

Backtrack to October of the same year.

At the time, I was self-employed, doing Internet marketing and consulting for small businesses. There's a perception that self-employment is the ultimate freedom. If done correctly, this can be true. In my situation, however, my so-called freedom translated to 70+ hours in front of my laptop each week. There was always something to be done. Since I didn't impose any sort of schedule upon myself, my default activity was work. Even when I did take a break from work, my form of escape was to browse Facebook, Twitter, write for my website, or watch Netflix. I was under the spell of the screen.

I could sense that my lifestyle was unsatisfying and unhealthy, both physically and mentally, but I was locked into a routine. The first thing I would do in the morning was roll over, open my laptop and check my e-mail. This was entirely subconscious. When I managed to pull myself away from the screen to go to the gym, for a hike, or for a run, I instantly felt better. Unfortunately those times were few and far between, and I'd be back in front of the screen before I knew it.

On one of the rare evenings where I decided to partake in social activity, I joined my friend, John, at the local watering hole. Everyone has that friend who is constantly organizing his/her next musical festival, vacation, party, and so on. John is my version of this friend. We were a few beers deep and he was updating me with the latest edition of his upcoming journeys.

"...and I know you'll like this one," John paused. His eyes grew wide. I knew something off the wall was to follow. "So there's this trail...."

John proceeded to inform me of his plans to thru-hike the AT- a 2,181-mile trip on a footpath that extends from Georgia to Maine! John had more camping experience than me, but not by a lot. To say that he was an experienced outdoorsman was a vast overstatement. At the time, John was working an IT job for a major golf equipment company. Much like myself, his competencies were behind a computer screen, not in the woods.

My stomach turned, I could feel an alarming energy overcome my body. The idea was insane, but on some level I knew this was the "out" I needed to catapult me from my unsatisfying routine.

"That's amazing. I'm coming with you."

And so it was set. Without having any idea what I was getting myself into, I verbally committed to the biggest adventure of my life.

Fast forward to January.

It was officially less than three months from my departure for the trail. My obsessive work ethic was dying, or more accurately, was being funneled into researching the trail. There was no shortage of information about thru-hiking online through various forums, websites, and blogs. These resources were helpful, but the quantity of advice was overwhelming, plus, opinions were often contradictory. Since I knew nothing, I had a lot of very specific questions. It quickly became clear that I was going to have trouble getting the right answers, or any answers at all.

As a result of some social media serendipity, I was put in touch with Josh Turner, who ran a video camping blog at the time called Camping Gear TV. Not only did Josh put me in contact with many of the sponsors of his show, which ultimately led to gear donations for John and me, but he connected me with Ian Mangiardi. Ian is a former AT and PCT thru-hiker[9]. In no uncertain terms, Ian became my thru-hike therapist/coach from that point until my departure for the trail.

In the process of talking me off the ledge several times as a result of severe pre-trail anxiety, Ian helped me to prepare mentally for what might occur over the next half year. More importantly Ian gave me tips on how to approach these challenging times. Up until this point, I had trouble finding information regarding the psychological battles I would confront along the trail. His forthrightness was a breath of fresh air.

Although I eventually altered Ian's advice to incorporate what I had already learned from reading dozens of books about human psychology and self-help, his words marked a sea change in my approach.

I was beginning to realize that if I had any shot of completing this thru-hike, I needed to prepare myself mentally. Instead of ignoring the obstacles ahead, I had to confront them now. More accurately, I had to confront myself. I accepted that my thru-hike was not only a geographical journey, but a personal one as well.

Instead of going on trial-run camping trips or spending hours deliberating about the perfect gear, I used my remaining time to focus on the gear between my ears. I predicted that building my mental muscle would build the endurance necessary for success.

My prediction proved correct.

Fast forward to April (On the trail for one month)

I had just returned from an unforeseen trip to Silicon Valley for a job interview with the only company on earth capable of enticing me off the trail (I'll elaborate in Chapter 6). By this point, the rest of my group was already one hundred miles ahead. I was now entirely by myself. Although I was a

---

[9] And the co-star of the PCT documentary, "As It Happens". If you haven't seen it, you're missing out. Go to http://bit.ly/AIH-movie

nervous about confronting the woods alone, I quickly proved to myself that this concern was unnecessary.

I was stealth camping in remote areas off the trail, building my own campfires, setting up my own bear-bags, and reaching a new height of affinity for my surroundings. I regularly went a full 48 hours before encountering another human being. Not only did I survive, I thrived. In just one month's time, I was a new person. At the very least, I was the same person with a radically new skill set. I had complete confidence in myself.

In the five months that it took me to complete the trail, I spent more time by myself than in the company of others. I had experiences that will live vividly in my mind until the day I die.

Without significant pre-trail preparation, it's safe to assume that I would have fallen into the unfortunate majority of hikers who drop off the trail. Wandering into the dark woods in the middle of nowhere by myself would have been enough for me to hit the panic button. As it turned out, I wasn't fazed in the least.

Instead, I would go on to tackle obstacles far greater than I could have ever predicted. Not once did I consider getting off the trail, even when my health began taking a turn for the worse (again, we'll cover this in Chapter 6). Instead, I spent most, though not all, of my days smiling. I attribute this entirely to the work I did before I ever left home.

By now you must be thinking, "Okay, great, so what is your advice? How can I mentally prepare myself?" Great question, that's the subject of our next chapter.

CHAPTER 2 -
MENTALLY PREPARING

Why prepare mentally for "a hike"? There are a lot of situations in life that require mental preparation- public speaking, a first date, attempting to lose a substantial amount of weight. *But a hike?* Really?

Really.

You've probably been on hikes before. Maybe you've backpacked. Perhaps you've even been on *extended* backpacking trips. You know what to expect. You wake up in your tent/shelter, eat, walk, poop, walk, eat, walk, eat, walk, poop, eat, set up camp, sleep, rinse and repeat. You probably didn't do any mental preparation and made it out just fine.

Non-competitive outdoor activities shouldn't require mental preparation. Such activities are typically done for leisure's sake. Backpacking is no exception. So why am I suggesting you do something that, at least on the surface, doesn't seem entirely necessary?

You know what you're giving up with your new lifestyle: a warm bed, a diet consisting of *real food*, regular access to a shower, electronic entertainment on demand, instant communication with friends, family, co-workers and so on. You wouldn't even consider hiking the Pacific Crest Trail if you hadn't come to grips with this. In fact, you're probably *excited* to do your best Thoreau impression and take part in a simpler, Walden-like lifestyle. *Minimally, you're not all that concerned about the lifestyle change.*

And for the first few weeks or so, you may question why I insisted that you prepare at all. After all, early on your hike will seem relatively effortless, at least from a psychological standpoint. The endorphins that accompany the increased heart rate offer a hiker's high for the bulk of the day. The breathtaking beauty of mountain and vast desert views, the escape from a rigid daily schedule will undoubtedly feel like a net lifestyle gain. But take note, the excitement will eventually fade, and when it does, you better be prepared.

For this reason, it's not the first month that you need to prepare for; *it's months two through five we're concerned with.*

In the beginning of your hike, everything will be exhilarating, even the hard times. Your first 90-degree day, the first time you wander off course, your first hailstorm, the first rattlesnake you narrowly avoid stepping on- situations that might arouse fear and/or frustration will leave you feeling on top of the world at the event's conclusion. There's a feeling of invincibility associated with overcoming these natural obstacles.

But, eventually aggravation replaces exhilaration (I will expand upon this later). While hiking through the heat of the desert may have been a fun, novel experience in the beginning, eventually your mind starts to say, "I'm hot. I'm drenched in sweat. My arms and hands are so burnt they look like lobster claws. I have blisters covering my feet. Heat rash has taken permanent residence on my body. Where the hell is the water? I could be home, chilling in the air conditioning, drinking beer while watching Game of Thrones from the comforts of my couch. ***Why am I doing this again?***"

This is a profound and *extremely* important question.

Why, exactly, *are you* doing this?

Since you *will* undoubtedly ask yourself this question, it's important to confront this *now*, so you have a compelling answer to give yourself not if, but when, this occurs.

You might be hesitant to simply take my word for it now, but please, take this seriously. There are countless former members of the military and experienced backpackers who throw in the towel on their thru-hike each year. Heck, there are former *thru-hikers* who quit on thru-hikes. These people aren't in over their heads. Their "*skill set*" is likely far ahead of yours. Certainly it was light years ahead of mine. Even from a mental fortitude standpoint, someone who's gone through the rigors of basic training can withstand a great deal of turmoil. They've gone through months, if not years, of grueling exercises and simulations to keep their mindset strong when shit hits the fan. So, how is it that someone of their ilk could cave in during what essentially amounts to a half-year vacation?

Because when it comes to backpacking 2,650 miles, the greatest determining factor of success is clarity of purpose.

In the throes of battle, (e.g. your third consecutive day of swimming in your own sweat from the relentless heat), it becomes much easier to forget *your* purpose. You'll remind yourself that hiking the PCT is a voluntary practice. No one is forcing you to do this. You're willingly walking through the rain, desert heat, and/or snow storm. To most, that's *insanity*. Right now, sitting on the couch, reading this book, the idea might seem fun. When your blisters outnumber your toes, it might not seem quite so fun. There will come a day when you ask yourself this all too important question. *Why am I doing this again?*

I was sure this day would come during my thru-hike. *Sure enough, it did.* Instead of being at the mercy of my emotions when it did, I needed a plan. I fully invested my emotions into building a compelling answer to this question before ever leaving for the trail. Zach needed to convince *Badger*[10] why he was doing what he was doing.

---

[10] What would eventually go onto become my trail name. In case you're wondering, there's no good story to accompany this; I chose a nickname that I already had. My reason for this was to keep it consistent with my website's name. If I could do it over again, I'd let the trail bestow my trail name organically.

So – I made lists.

> *"If you don't know where you are going, you might wind up someplace else."* – **Yogi Berra**

The first list, entitled *"I am Thru-Hiking the Appalachian Trail because..."* focused solely on the *why*. This and all of the subsequent titles were positively stated to reinforce my conviction in finishing.

Here are some of the examples from my list:

<u>I am Thru- Hiking the Appalachian Trail because...</u>

- – I need some time to re-evaluate the direction of my career
- – I am craving an adventure larger than life
- – Life is short, do awesome shit, stupid
- – Postponing happiness until retirement is a flawed life approach
- – I have the rest of my life to sit in front of a computer
- – I want to expose myself to a new environment
- – I need a change of pace
- – What I'm currently doing isn't working
- – I suck at backpacking

The second list, entitled *"When I Successfully Thru-Hike the Appalachian Trail, I will..."* focused on the personal benefits I hoped to acquire from thru-hiking the trail. I imagined a set of rewards waiting for me at the northern terminus, like presents sitting under a Christmas tree. Although it's silly, it got me where I wanted to go. Additionally, I can say with conviction that each of these "presents" are now in my possession. They are:

<u>When I successfully thru-hike the Appalachian Trail, I will...</u>

- – have an unshakeable confidence
- – have the story of a lifetime
- – restore a clearer sense of presence

- turn a glaring weakness into a strength
- see life in a new light
- have overcome the greatest challenge of my life
- be a better listener
- leverage this accomplishment to create
  new momentum
- have a clearer idea of what I want to do in life

I don't think I'm going out on a limb by saying that you have your own compelling reasons for hiking the PCT[11]. Maybe you're unsatisfied with the current direction that your life is heading. Maybe you're seeking a change of pace or a new challenge. Maybe you're an adventure junkie and the PCT is your crown jewel. Perhaps thru-hiking the Pacific Crest Trail is something you've wanted to do for *many* years, but haven't been able to find the time and/or money to take it on, and now you do. Whatever the reason, take some time to consider *why* you're *really* doing this[12]. Remember, there will come a time when you will ask yourself this very question. Show me someone without a compelling answer and I'll show you someone who will eventually be homebound.

Take *at least* twenty to thirty minutes to consider all of the reasons you want to hike the Pacific Crest Trail. Include as many benefits as you can possibly anticipate getting out of hiking the trail. Be honest with yourself. The PCT is unique opportunity for growth. Failing to take advantage of this is a mistake. What sorts of changes would you like to see in your life?

It likely goes without saying, but your lists will replace the Appalachian Trail with the Pacific Crest Trail from the examples above. I've included a series of template lists for you to use in the appendices of this book. If you'd rather not rip pages out of this book, or are working on an e-reader, I've also made printable .pdf versions available on at the following address: **http://bit.ly/why-hike**

---

[11] If your reason is "because Cheryl Strayed did", keep digging.

[12] Ryan, R.M., & Deci, E.L. (2000). Self-determination theory and facilitation of intrinsic motivation, social development, and well-being. American Psychologist, 55, 68-78.

Commit your responses to writing. *Do it now.*
...
Seriously. Do it.
...
I'm not kidding.
...
Now.
...
I'll wait.
...
(...humming Taylor Swift songs...)
...
(*"Cause a player's gunna play, play, play, play, play...."*)
...
(*"...Shake it off. A'shake it off...."*)
...
Ok, you did it?
...
Good.

Your list will be a powerful tool to keep you motivated during your *Pacific Crest trials*. However, focusing on the positive traits that you'll acquire upon finishing is only half the battle. You also need to create a list of *negative* consequences associated with *quitting* on the trail[13].

   This list is titled *"If I give up on the Pacific Crest Trail, I will..."* The following are some examples from my list.

If I give up on the Appalachian Trail, I will...

   – never believe in myself
   – not like the person I see in the mirror
   – continue to settle in all other aspects of my life (career wise, physically, relationships, etc.)
   – not be the person I believe that I am
   – carry the baggage of shame
   – reveal my lack of confidence in my posture

---

[13] Jones, M.V. (2012). Emotional regulation and performance. In S.M. Murphy (Ed.), The Oxford Handbook of Sport and Performance Psychology (pp.154-172). New York: Oxford University Press.

– not be able to attract others

Again, take *at least* twenty minutes to consider all the potential consequences of giving up on your goal. Really put yourself into the mental/emotional state of how you'll feel if you don't follow through. How will you cope with this? Will you start eating/drinking more? Will you slack off in your career? What other areas of your life will you start compromising? How will you treat those around you? What effect will that have on your relationships? What will your skeptics think of you?[14] *Go deep.*[15]

Write down everything you feel. Err on the side of being too descriptive and/or redundant rather than being brief.

Bring these lists with you. Every time you sense yourself starting to slip emotionally, pull out your lists and review them. Better yet, don't let yourself get to that point. Remind yourself as often as possible. Every two weeks, every week, every day. The work you do with this before you leave for the trail may very well be the difference between Canada and quitting. At the very least, it will help to boost your spirits, even if you aren't at the point where you're contemplating vacating the trail.

I reviewed my lists once a week before I fell asleep. Not only did this help in keeping me determined, it also served as a reminder of what I was originally looking to get from the trip. You have plenty of free time on the trail. You'll never have a better opportunity to clear your head and re-install new software, or at least clean out the viruses.

The above lists are only the first step in your pre-trail work. Now, let's step it up a notch.

This following step is *crazy* important. I'm talking Gary Busey crazy.

---

[14] This may seem like a superficial concern; it is. Realistically, the outside world's view of us can be a powerful motivator. Use that to your advantage. If you're able to rise above and not care what others think, more power to you. I'd venture to guess that most do not fall in this category.

[15] Benson, A.J., Evans, B.E., Surya, M., Martin, L.J., & Eys, M.A. (2015). Embracing athletic identity in the face of threat. Sport, Exercise, and Performance Psychology, 4, 303-315.

Publicly state your mission.

You're about to embark on something truly epic, now is no time to be bashful. You are going to *walk* from Mexico to Canada. Let people know! Tell friends. Tell family. Tell co-workers. Tell neighbors. Tell the barista at Starbucks. Tell your mailman. Tell your hair stylist/barber. Tell your pets. Tell Facebook. Tell Twitter, Instagram, Snapchat, and whatever else the kids are using these days. Do you have a website? Yes? Announce it there. No? Step 1: Start one.[16] Step 2: TELL PEOPLE!

Publicly announcing your thru-hike is crucial for two reasons. First, it makes your plan more real. Seeing the reactions in others will help to put into perspective how truly monumental your goal really is! Secondly, and more importantly, it makes you accountable. More accurately, others will hold you accountable. If you want to back out of the trail at any point, not only do you have to look yourself in the mirror, but you'll have a lot of people to answer to. Oftentimes, the shame associated with coming back home with your tail between your legs will be enough motivation to keep you going. Use this social pressure in your favor[17].

This tactic helped me immensely. When I announced to my family that I was going to thru-hike the Appalachian Trail, they only took me half seriously. They knew that I wasn't exactly the *outdoorsy* type. Time and again, I would bring up the fact that I was planning on hiking from Georgia to Maine, and I could see their eyes glaze over. It wasn't until I wrote a post announcing my plans to thru-hike on theGoodBadger.com (my personal website) that they took me seriously. They knew more than anyone else how much I value my site and its readers. Although they thought maybe I was just blowing smoke up the collective family butt, there was no way I would bullshit my readers.

---

[16] Or save yourself the hassle and join our blogging team at bit.ly/PCTblogger

[17] Marchant, D.B. (2000). Targeting futures: Goal setting for professional sports. In M.B. Andersen (Ed.), Doing Sport Psychology (pp. 93-103). Champaign, IL: Human Kinetics.

It was at that exact moment where my mom's anxiety level escalated into red, and would hover near the *panic zone* until the day I completed my thru-hike.

Additionally, all of my friends knew about this. I had a going away party in both San Diego and Chicago.[18] I couldn't imagine coming back and looking these people in the eyes saying, "Yeah, well, I tried, but it was *really* hard. I'm sure you understand." Having to explain my failure seemed far more difficult than walking.

In retrospect, I'm very happy that publicly announced my intent to thru-hike. You will be too, *trust me.*

Wanna make a bet?

In the process of telling people that you're going on a 2,650-mile hike, you will likely encounter a few skeptics along the way. As you might guess, I had more than my fair share. Although it may seem like an attempt to shake your confidence, their skepticism can be a powerful tool to further motivate yourself.

Instead of getting defensive, or questioning yourself, test *their* confidence. Find out exactly *how sure* they are of your failure by asking them to put their money where their *nay-saying* mouth is. Remind them that only a fraction of attempting thru-hikers end up finishing (you know, to get better odds).

Not only is betting on yourself a powerful tactic for motivation, it also takes advantage of a trait ingrained in all humans: aversion to loss. We hate losing. We hate losing even more than we *love* winning.[19] By making some sort of

---

[18] And by "party", I mean imbibing with friends while they try to convince me that I was a dead man.

[19] Gächter S., Johnson, Eric J., Herrmann A., (2010, November 16). Individual-level loss aversion in riskless and risky choices. Retrieved from: http://cess.nyu.edu/schotter/wp-content/uploads/2010/02/%E2%80%9CUnderstanding-Overbidding-Using-the-Neural-Circuitry-of-Reward-to-Design-Economic-Auctions%E2%80%9D.pdf

monetary wager on your success, the loss associated with not finishing will be more tangible and motivating.[20]

Acceptance

The final step in your mental preparation is an important one: *acceptance.*

If your pre-hike emotional state is any anything like mine was, you might be a tad on the anxious side.[21] Instead of trying to fight these feelings, allow them to occur freely, and more importantly, don't let them dissuade you from the trail[22]. Not only is this perfectly normal, it's healthy. Nervous energy is a common precursor to positive change. You've probably already experienced similar emotions during another transitional phase in your life, whether it be going away to college, moving to a new city, ending a bad relationship, changing careers and so on. I'm guessing the change was necessary to your life, and ultimately had a positive outcome. The trail is no different. You have good reasons for hiking the Pacific Crest Trail. If you don't believe me, consult your lists.

It might be helpful to write your pre-trail feelings down. For starters, it's therapeutic. Putting your emotions into words will help to diffuse the negative energy[23]. Also, once you have successfully completed the trail, your writing will provide a powerful barometer that will allow you to see how far you've come. It will help you gauge how much you have grown as a person.

---

[20] Standage, M., & Ryan, R.M. (2012). Self-determination theory and exercise motivation: Facilitating self-regulatory processes to support and maintain health and well-being. In G.C. Roberts & D.C. Treasure (Eds.), Advances in motivation in sport and exercise (3rd ed., pp. 233-270). Champaign, IL: Human Kinetics.

[21] Understatement of the millennium. I'm pretty sure I slept for a total of 85 minutes total in the final month leading up to the trail. I could've easily fit all of my gear in the bags under my eyes.

[22] Luoma, J.B., Hayes, S.C., & Walser, R.D. (2007). Learning ACT: An acceptance and commitment therapy skills-training manual for therapists. Oakland, CA: New Harbinger Publications.

[23] Lazarus, R.S., & Folkman, S. (1984). Stress, appraisal, and coping. New York: Spring Publishing Company.

Summary

By following through with the above steps, you will be light-years ahead of others in your quest to successfully thru-hike the PCT. More importantly, you will be prepared when you encounter your first set of Pacific Crest trials. And I have a good guess precisely *where* that will happen. But before we get to that, let's look at what you can expect at *the beginning* of the trail.

SECTION TWO:
ON TRAIL

Chapter 3 - The Beginning

You've finally done it. All your hard work prior to leaving has led up to this moment: you've made it to Campo, you're minutes away from the Mexico / United States border and the start of your life-changing journey.

You're at the beginning. You realize there's a great deal ahead of you, but at last you are finally walking to Canada!

The question now becomes, *what happens to your mental state once on the trail?* If there is one thing you need to know about these early stages of the trail, it's that you're stepping foot on to...

The Pacific Crest Roller Coaster

My Early Ups and Downs, *by Carly Moree*

We were told to expect forty miles with no water.

Three in the morning came too quickly. The night before, I along with two other thru-hikers, Jeffe and Chickenfat, decided that we would hike this full stretch in one day, partially for the challenge, partially for "fun", partially due to the lack of water. Rumor on the trail was there might be a pair of water caches between Landers Meadow and Walker Pass campground, but as I had already learned, relying on "maybes" was a fool's game.

My watch alarm buzzed me awake at 3:00 am on the dot. We still had nearly two hours before we'd see any daylight. Packing up camp was slow going. Our brains were still asleep, but we were also dreading the distance we'd have to cover and the amount of water we'd have to haul in the process.

An hour later, we were on trail. My premonition proved correct, carrying six liters of water felt as if someone had slipped a bowling ball in my bag[24]. As soon as the sun came up, it was apparent that the day was going to be a burner, typical for the southern California desert in June.

After several miles of meandering around desert shrub under a punishing, cloudless blue sky, we happened upon the first water cache. There sat more than 20 plastic jugs filled with water next to a dirt road. Although this victory didn't lighten our load, it allowed us to camel up on water, which served as a massive morale boost. When covering long waterless stretches, you drink only as much water as you need, not as much as you want. With this bonus water, we were able to throttle back from survival mode. To celebrate this victory, Chickenfat shared some of his coffee candy. Things were looking up.

Before the taste of caffeinated candy had left my mouth, I was already drenched in my own sweat. Some say that girls don't sweat, they glisten. I have to believe these sweat-free ladies have never hiked through the Southern California desert in summer, because under this punishing Mojave sun, *everyone sweats*. Hot air engulfed us. Sunlight blanketed the expansive desert terrain as far as the eye could see.

It was only a couple hours after our water cache reprieve that my body started to break down. Despite drinking plenty of water, I felt sick- nauseous, dizzy, and with a throbbing headache. It felt like the sun was cooking my brain. My sweat soaked shirt stuck to my skin like a suction cup. Sunscreen and sweat were cascading down my bright red, sun-cooked calves. While dragging my feet up a

---

[24] In fact, six liters of water equals 13.2 pounds. Staying hydrated is heavy.

mild-ascent, a climb made exponentially more difficult by the heat, all I could wonder was, "Is this what heat stroke feels like? Am I going to make it to the next water cache? *Is there* another water cache?"

Outwardly I was calm, I didn't want to alarm my hiking partners. On the inside, however, I was a mess. The heat was zapping my energy along with my sanity.

Then, just as my spirits were about to dip below the desert valley, I saw it. First the tent, next the gallons of water safely tucked away in the shade, then the folding chairs, you know the type - the ones you might bring to your nephew / niece's youth soccer game, and the cooler full of snacks. Trail magic! We collapsed into the chairs, each seeking refuge under the shade. My worries evaporated, as did the sweat drenching my clothes and coating my skin. As we sat drinking water and eating peanut butter tortillas, we joked about the last things we would ever want or need at a cache in the desert (a game which we cleverly dubbed, "Desert Cache").

"Hot sauce! And those big aluminum-wrapped boards you can tan yourself with," I said in between bites of lunch.

"A bag of concrete mix," added Chickenfat.

Just thirty minutes prior, I was worried I was about to succumb to heat stroke. Now, I was all smiles, laughing along with my fellow desert comrades.

After a couple hours of escaping the sun, we were back at it. With each switchback leading up Walker Pass, I was gaining strength. Nearing the top, I turned my head to take in the vast Mojave Desert view, only to see gray clouds filling the sky above me. I had already been rained on several times, despite multiple people assuring me they hardly saw any rain through this southern section. There was no way I was about to get served *another* storm.

Ten minutes later, it was storming. We were under freezing rain and half-dollar sized hail, which pelted my arms and neck, resulting in welts. We came to a dirt road where the trail turned left. Or was it right? There was no trail marker, or at least not easily visible when you're turtled up in rain gear, and no one wanted to take out their phone to check the GPS, so we *guessed* left. We hiked fifteen more minutes without any clear indication that we made the right decision. Eventually Chickenfat pulled out his phone, fired up the Guthook PCT app, and confirmed we had guessed correctly. As I stood there waiting for Chickenfat to check our course, I was shivering. Earlier in the day, I was concerned I had heat stroke. Now I was worried about hypothermia?!

We continued to trudge through puddles.

When the storm finally stopped, I was exhausted and soaked. With only a few miles left until we reached the Walker Pass campground, the evening sun finally broke through the clouds. We took a quick break to eat, drink, and dry out our soaked clothes and dampened morale. We were quiet, tired, famished, and dehydrated. Words were sparse as we picked through our trail mix.

As Jeffe stood up to continue on, Chickenfat frantically pointed at his pants and yelled, "Jeffe!". Jeffe had apparently sat in an ant hill, as evidenced by the seemingly millions of tiny, black insects inhabiting his lower half. In all my life, I've never seen so many ants. None of us, Jeffe included, could stop laughing as he danced around and hysterically tried to brush them off.

After Jeffe's ants pants dance, we began our final push of the day. Our spirits were high again. We talked and laughed as we descended to the campground. We set up camp next to a picnic table, where we ate our staple hiker dinner of dehydrated pastas, tuna and mashed potatoes. As I lay in my sleeping bag, cowgirl-camping[25] under the star-filled sky, all I could think about was how thankful I was to be dry and not moving. I began to replay the day's events. Heat stroke and hypothermia. Delight and defeat. Trail magic and trials. Extreme highs and lows. We had all just taken our first ride on the Pacific Crest Roller Coaster.

So what can you take away from the above story?

The PCT has lows

---

[25] Cowgirl or cowboy camping refers to sleeping without a shelter. Just a sleeping bag and pad under the stars.

You won't be on the trail long before you learn that you're at the mercy of Mother Nature; she will have her way with you. Climbing out of your sleeping bag before sunrise will expose you to her surprisingly frigid air. Eventually the sun will climb above the horizon and within a couple of hours, sweat will permeate every inch of your clothing. You'll feel as if you're hiking in an oven- set to whatever temperature is optimal for cooking hiker casserole. You carefully ration each sip of water, knowing that you get only 1.5 liters over the next 10 miles. Just when you think it can't get any worse, a hailstorm quickly swoops in and pummels your head and neck. You're now longing for the ungodly heat you had just sworn off. You're somehow wet and dehydrated, cold and sun burnt.

The PCT has highs

Eventually, however, Mother Nature will come around. The clouds will clear, the sun will appear, and she will smile down upon you.

Regardless of the elements, you will find respite from the chaos in due time. You'll reach the campsite and run into other hikers who have just fought the same battle. You and your fellow PCT-mates will commiserate over what you've just gone through. The trials are what causes a unique and strong community to build. Someone in the group will offer up their cigarette, spliff, or whiskey flask. Your nerves will settle and all that remains will be residual adrenaline. You will be left with a sense of invincibility. You'll have proven to yourself that, although the elements may be challenging, it's a challenge that you can overcome.

Or maybe you'll get to town. You'll hit that cafe and down a double bacon cheeseburger and plate of chili cheese fries. Better add a milkshake and a beer. You earned it. You'll grab a shower. Doing your laundry will seem like a reward rather than a chore. You will have a newfound appreciation for the small things in life you once took for granted.

Hiking the Pacific Crest Trail is a lesson in volatility. Just when you think things are at their worst, serendipity will strike, and your day will turn around. Like riding a roller coaster, the motions are out of your control. Your only job is to enjoy the ride.

Some context

To clarify- not every day during this initial stretch will be a roller coaster. Some days, will be normal, peaceful days- walking through moderate temperature, dry conditions with *enough* access to water.

The point is that in relation to the rest of the trail, this initial period will present higher highs and lower lows. Although you will experience new microclimates as you progress north, this initial stretch will be the period where you're still acclimating to a life outdoors. The remainder of your experience on trail stabilizes, not because the intensity of external events lets up- in fact, in any given year, they can increase- but because you eventually adapt. For this reason, the ups and downs will have a much more profound effect on you early on. The challenges you encounter in the desert will better prepare you for what lurks in the Sierra and beyond, even if they have little in common.

And because this period is such a roller coaster ride, it is my opinion this initial stage is actually *easier* than the rest of the trail. Over time you will be better equipped to handle these various lows – extreme physical discomfort, wandering off trail, the lightning storms, misjudging and consequently rationing your water supply – and the rush of adrenaline associated with overcoming these obstacles will be replaced by irritation. In the beginning, though, the challenges will be hard, but they'll be temporarily exciting.

So what will the beginning of the trail be like for you?

All that we can say with confidence is that the pendulum swing is more extreme. If you're not an experienced backpacker, there's no way you'll know exactly what to expect on the Pacific Crest roller coaster. Every day is an adventure. Even if it's difficult, it's thrilling. If you can't get up for that, the Pacific Crest Trail probably isn't for you.

Also, keep in mind that these early hills and valleys are where you develop a sense of appreciation. This is a huge part of the trail. Walking in the relentless heat for hours is what makes sitting in a shade-covered chair with friends by your side a gift. Getting pummeled by hail is what makes the returning desert sunshine a welcomed sight. Hiking through an allegedly waterless stretch is what makes coming across gallons of water generously provided by total strangers feel like pure euphoria. Exerting all your energy to survive the day is what makes sitting on a rusty picnic table, eating mashed potatoes for the fifth night in a row such a treat. Exposing yourself to these elements is what makes the refuge that follows so enjoyable. A deprivation lifestyle gives us the opportunity to fully appreciate *what we do have*. This is what hiking the Pacific Crest Trail is all about.

Why People Drop Out Early

Although there are no official records for thru-hiker completion rates on the PCT, the Pacific Crest Trail Association (PCTA), the nonprofit overseeing the trail, used to state that, "Approximately 50% of those who start a thru-hike, finish"[26]. Hikethrough.com ran an analysis that found the thru-hiker completion rate is closer to 40%[27]. In any case, best estimates say that the odds are somewhere between a coin flip and "not good". I predict that the completion rates will drop even lower as more first-time thru-hikers hit the PCT, a byproduct of the "*Wild* Effect", the growth in interest of the PCT due to the book and movie *Wild*.

Nevertheless, the completion rates are significantly lower than 100%, and many of those who drop off are going to do so before they get out of the desert.

In 2014, one hiker was rescued on his fourth day on trail, only 15 miles north of Campo. He was carrying what was estimated as a 65 lb. pack and ran out of water on his second day. He was found laying under a bush in an effort

---

[26] Long-distance hiking. (n.d.). Retrieved January 10, 2016, from http://www.pcta.org/discover-the-trail/long-distance-hiking/

[27] Thru-Hike Success Rate. (2009). Retrieved February 10, 2016, from http://hikethru.com/about-the-pct/thru-hike-success-rate

to stay out of the sun[28]. We're not sure if this hiker ended up getting off the trail permanently or not, but that's not a promising start.

David "ChinMusic" Milner, was another such example. Despite successfully thru-hiking the AT in 2013, ChinMusic didn't make it out of the Mojave before throwing in the towel during his 2015 attempted thru-hike. The reason? He didn't have anything left to prove to himself. As he puts it:

> *"[After completing the AT] the monkey was off my back. Would I have that same burning desire to complete another thru? It was that burning desire that kept me going on the AT; it was my friend and constant companion...I can't but help but believe that my lack of burning desire to do the PCT contributed [to my quitting]. "*

So, despite the above stories, how can we claim that hiking the Pacific Crest Trail is actually easiest in its early stages? There are two primary reasons we believe people vacate the trail early on, and a few others worth at least considering.

1) People push themselves past their limits.

Although starting the trail in great shape will be a tremendous advantage, it is by no means a prerequisite. You can begin the Pacific Crest Trail in less than prime condition[29]. That said, a solid cardiovascular foundation will serve to ease your transition to the thru-hiking lifestyle,

---

[28] Rescue at Hauser Canyon. (2014, March 26). Retrieved January 12, 2016, from https://blondiehikes.wordpress.com/2014/03/26/rescue-at-hauser-canyon/

[29] If you're in horrendous shape, then you have a problem. You have approximately five snow-free months to complete a NOBO thru-hike. This amounts to a 21.4-mile per day average assuming you take one zero every week. If you come onto the PCT in poor fitness, you'll come nowhere close to this daily mileage out the gate. This can make you feel as if you're playing catch up during the rest of your journey, which can be a major stressor.

thus making it far less likely for you to get frustrated and drop out.

Regardless of your starting condition, you can- and should- consider the first three to five weeks of the trail your training for the remainder of your hike. Your fitness should dictate your initial level of output. If you go on the trail as someone who regularly competes in Ironman races, you probably don't have to hold back all that much. If you're the type who feels destroyed after a two-mile jog, you need to be extra cautious. Most people will fall somewhere in between these points on the spectrum.

To be clear, I don't recommend going into the trail in poor shape. I'm not a doctor, nor do I play one in books, but if you're a bona fide couch potato, exerting yourself in the extreme desert heat can pose very serious health risks. If you're not confident in your ability to shoulder more than 25 lbs. through the heat, seek the input of a medical practitioner. Older hikers should also take greater precaution before setting out for the trail. Additionally, if you're hoping for a continuous NOBO thru-hike, you'll *only* have about a five-month window before winter becomes too big of a threat in Washington. The overall point still stands- if you're not in great shape, you can still successfully thru-hike, you will just have more of an adjustment early on.

The best piece of advice we can offer for this initial stretch is to cover less ground than you feel you're capable of. This beginning stage is the point where you're the most injury-prone. Unless you've done a lot of sport-specific training before hitting the trail, there's no way you can, nor should, hit the ground running. Your muscles, tendons, ligaments and joints will take a serious beating. Your feet will swell and flatten. Your body will go into shock. You will wake up sore, and without ample rest, the pain begins to accumulate. Trying to push yourself through this pain is what pushes many people off the trail early on.

One such cautionary tale comes from Anna "Jolly" Marini's attempted thru-hike in 2015. Ending her hike in Wrightwood, California was not what she had planned, but after almost 400 miles of constant pain in her feet, Jolly made the decision to pull the plug. In her own words,

"I definitely pushed myself too hard in the beginning. I wanted to keep up with the other hikers around me, everyone was so excited to get started and move on to the next town. I should have listened to my body and let myself get used to hiking every day."

If you're the type who'll be tempted to keep pace with the crowd (which is a common mistake, we will cover in Chapter 5), then it's in your best interest to arrive at Campo in great backpacking shape. If you're not in great shape, be prepared to watch your early hiking companions pass you by.

Advil is an extremely common substance on the trail for this reason. It's not uncommon for people to take up the to six to eight pills per day. Because ibuprofen (referred to as "Vitamin I" in the endurance sports world) is an anti-inflammatory, it will reduce swelling, thus making your hike more bearable. However, never take any medication, prescribed or over-the-counter, to mask pain in order to continue hiking. Pain is your body's way of telling you that something is wrong. Ignoring this signal is a one-way ticket to Injuryville, population: you. Keep this in mind.

Those are the *physical* reasons for not pushing yourself excessively in the beginning. From a psychological standpoint, you will need to develop a marathon mentality (covered in chapter 8) if you plan on succeeding. Pushing yourself to the limit in these early stages, even if you are able to stave off injury, will prove to be a dangerous approach in regards to your sanity. Canada is a long ways off. A long, long, long ways off. Cool your jets, friend. You'll get there. Be patient.

As a general precaution, treat the first three weeks of your thru-hike as your adaptation period. If you're in poor shape, start with 8-12 miles a day . If you're in good shape, start with 15-20 miles per day. Many hikers attempt to reach the campground at Lake Morena 20 miles from the southern terminus on their first day. For those who aren't in prime hiking condition, this is likely a mistake. Again, it's good psychological training to resist the urge to follow the crowd and instead listen to your own body.

If, after a few days, your body is relatively pain-free, start to slowly increase your mileage. There's no penalty for doing too few miles. The punishment for hiking too many, however, is severe. If your body starts to exhibit signs of wearing down, scale back your miles and/or take a zero or two. Remember that you are at your most fragile right now. You will get to the point where you will be the hiking version of Robocop, but it will take some time to get there. Don't let your ego prevent you from achieving your goal.

The last thing you want to do is fall victim to the PCT in the first two or three weeks because you were impatient. Be good to your body, you will be asking a lot of it in the months to come.

2) People who never took the emotional and psychological battles seriously

Because you've picked up this book and followed through with all of the steps indicated in the preparation chapter, you are not someone who has minimized the emotional and psychological battles. You realize that, although a half-year backpacking trip will be an overdose of fun, it's also challenging beyond belief. You take thru-hiking seriously. You accept that with the good will come the bad. You want to be prepared for when the bad happens so you can persevere. You're taking the necessary steps to do this the right way.

Not everyone is like you though.

A lot of people like the idea of a long, exciting adventure. They like to tell people that they're going to accomplish something as incredible as walking from Mexico to Canada. They're convinced they're prepared because they've spent a good amount of time outdoors. They went on a weekend backpacking trip, once. Their cousin showed them how to throw a hatchet. They joined a CrossFit gym and they can now kettlebell swing their pack clean over the nearest mountain.

They're way ahead of the game.

Truth be told, people like this haven't put enough thought into how difficult five months in the backcountry really is. As soon as they are confronted with their first lightning storm, they'll think back to their comfy leather couch, Apple TV, and the new pizza joint that just opened down the street. They'll report back to their friends that the PCT is impossible and that only a madman is capable of finishing such a trek.

The reality is, people like this failed before they ever left for the trail. Although they spent hours on end researching every piece of gear in their pack, they missed the mark. They prepared themselves for a physical fight, but ultimately lost the mental battle. They finally learned what you already know: comparing a weekend backpacking trip to thru-hiking the PCT is like comparing stubbing your toe to birthing triplets.

In my opinion, those who drop out in the first couple of weeks (barring serious injury, illness, or other similar unforeseen tragedy) never really stood a chance to thru-hike in the first place.

Additional Considerations

Although the above reasons seem to be the most common struggles for hikers early on, there are other pitfalls to guard yourself against during this initial stretch.

3) Significant other withdrawal

This issue will be especially true if you're the type of person who spends every free minute with your partner. Going from being connected at the hip to your girlfriend, boyfriend or spouse, to living without this person in the wilderness is likely going to be a shock to the psyche.

If this describes your situation, you're going to have more working against you than your fellow, non-romantically-involved hikers. Because both Carly and I went into our thru-hikes as single as can be, we cannot offer any first hand advice. In talking to others who were going through this, however, it did seem that the struggle lessened with time. They made a point to call their partner whenever in town, they sent postcards regularly, and were visited by their loved ones at least once during their thru-hike.

The times when the significant other withdrawal flared up was during the hiker's struggles on the trail. In other words, the struggle triggered feelings of withdrawal, not the other way around. Because of this, it seems that the best strategy to stave off separation anxiety is to do your best damn job to enjoy the trail as much as possible – your ultimate goal anyway.

For those going onto the trail with a spouse or serious relationship, I encourage you to check out Ashli Baldwin's wonderful article "12 Tips for Thru-Hikers Separated from Their Spouse" at http://bit.ly/SignificantOtherPCT.

4) Sticking with the wrong group

Most people will want to hike with others, especially in the beginning. However, getting caught up in a group with whom you don't mesh well can be difficult, to say the least. Whether it's mismatched hiking pace or personality differences, adding social struggles to these early stages can be the difference between loving and hating the trail. Most people quickly realize this and do their own thing or find other groups with whom to spend their time. Some, however, stick with the first group they meet. In their case, familiarity trumps compatibility.

I will address the social aspect of the trail in more depth in Chapter 5, but for now, the only thing you need to keep in mind is that you're better off by yourself than with a group you don't like. The PCT is chock-full of truly awesome people, so odds are that you'll quickly find a group that's a better fit, but this may require venturing off on your own for a bit.

Remember, you're in charge of making the most of your time. If something isn't working for you, *change it.*

5) Improper gear

Not carrying a bear canister in the High Sierra will result in a fine. Not having sun protection in the desert will bring you pain. Not having a sufficiently warm sleep system can cost your life. Since purchasing the proper equipment seems to be people's biggest focus, improper gear is not the reason *most* people drop out. However, if you haven't done your homework regarding acquiring the appropriate gear, you could face serious fines, extreme discomfort, and/or death[30].

Another aspect to consider is the weather variability from one year to the next. Looking at one year's weather conditions and expecting your year to offer the same is a mistake. In 2010-2011, the Sierra Nevada saw near record snowfall[31]. The next four years, this same region suffered through a drought[32]. Some years, the desert sees very little precipitation. Sometimes you encounter multiple hailstorms, as Carly did. Some years Washington is very wet. Other years, the state is on fire. The point is, in order to complete a PCT thru-hike, you'll need gear suitable for a variety of conditions.

If you haven't done your research, don't fret because we've got an excellent gear chapter in the bonus section of this book.

Final thought

The key point of preparation in regards to this early stretch is to enjoy the bejesus out of it. For those who are relatively new to backpacking, this will be the most exciting part of

---

[30] Death as a means of avoiding a fine is not recommended.

[31] Zito, K. (2011, March 30). Sierra snowpack is one of biggest on record. Retrieved January 12, 2016, from http://www.sfgate.com/green/article/Sierra-snowpack-is-one-of-biggest-on-record-2376945.php

[32] Burt, C. C. (2014, January 15). Central California Enters a Drought Period Unprecedented in its Weather History. Retrieved January 10, 2016, from http://www.wunderground.com/blog/weatherhistorian/comment.html?entrynum=233

trail. Don't take that for granted. Live every day to its fullest. Explore. Meet new people. Learn new backcountry tricks from others. Take copious amounts of photos. Keep a journal to record everything that's happening. When you read through it five, ten, or twenty years after finishing the trail, your notes will be a time machine transporting you back to this surreal period of your life.

After this bliss, you are going to face a time when, *rumor has it*, the trail begins to lose its luster. And this is the subject of the next chapter, The Death of the Honeymoon.

CHAPTER 4 - THE DEATH OF THE HONEYMOON

A s we pointed out in the previous chapter, your first month (or so) on the trail will be unfiltered insanity, *especially* if this is your first long distance trek. We mean that in the best way possible. Practically everything is so exciting and new that you will require little guidance in terms of staying positive. Excitement has a tendency to make the hands on your watch spin a little faster. The first month will be gone before you know it. Take this as your reminder to enjoy this early period as much as possible.

Which bring us to our point....

On the Appalachian Trail, there is a phenomenon known as the Virginia Blues. As the name implies, the Virginia Blues is a momentary stint of depression caused by the fact that Virginia never seems to end and the (mis)perception of repetitive scenery throughout the state, referred to as the green tunnel. Hikers experience the *Groundhog Day*[33] effect whereby every morning seems to bring the same location, time, and situation.

---

[33] In case you're unfamiliar, *Groundhog Day* is a movie starring Bill Murray. The movie was filmed in my hometown, Woodstock, IL. I had to find a way to work that into the book. End shameless plug.

On the PCT, there is no phenomenon known as the California Blues. Nearly two thirds of the entire trail runs through California. If it were the case that well over half of this journey would bring about "the blues", it's safe to assume that fewer people would enlist. Also consider that thru-hikers cross only two state lines during their entire journey. While crossing into a new state is exciting, PCT hikers don't rely so heavily on them as markers of accomplishment. And although the state remains the same, hikers seemingly walk into a new world when crossing from the desert into the High Sierra, and then again when leaving the Sierra. State boundaries are just invisible lines on a map, this ecological and geographical shift is far more palpable.

That said, it *is* common for many thru-hikers' spirits to take a serious dip while in the state of California. In the case of the PCT, this has nothing to do with the number of miles spent in the same state. This has nothing to do with lackluster scenery. It has everything to do with the death of the honeymoon.

The Honeymoon

As we mentioned previously, the beginning of your trip is going to be chocolate-covered chaos. You will wake up in a pure state of anticipation, excited for the day's events. For those with little to no backpacking experience, each climb, each Snicker's break, each snake encounter, each hitchhike, will prove to be nothing short of exhilarating. Every person you encounter will embody this energy, compounding your excitement. You will think back to your former life- a time when the most exciting part of your day was measured in "Likes", inside a 12-ounce can, or was preceded by "http://". In no uncertain terms, you will be in love with the Pacific Crest Trail, and the Pacific Crest Trail will be in love with you.

Chances are you've experienced this before, maybe not the equivalent of an extended backpacking trip, but a sense of infatuation in a different context. Maybe it was a new relationship, an extended stay abroad, moving to a new city, the purchase of a coveted possession, the transition to a new career path, and so on. At first there's a feeling of everything being right in the world. Nothing can touch you; you've finally found a way to keep your brain in a state of dopamine saturation. You walk with an extra skip in your step. You smile at strangers. You hum songs you don't even like. If there were babies around, you would kiss them. *You are in the honeymoon phase.*

And then, things change. That new car soon becomes last year's model and is no longer a source of pride. Your new boyfriend/girlfriend is beginning to reveal his or her flaws, or more accurately, you're allowing yourself to notice them. The new city that once offered an ocean of unlimited adventure suddenly doesn't seem so big; you've been to every venue, eaten at every restaurant, and you're once again locked into your set of routines. You already know this feeling. It's the death of the honeymoon.

R.I.P. Honeymoon

This transition is normal; thru-hiking the Pacific Crest Trail is not exempt from it.

For some hikers, this dip in spirits will happen during the first three to six weeks, coinciding with their time in the desert. Logically, hikers may assume that the alleged repetitive scenery is the cause. In fact, blaming the desert for your melancholy makes as much sense as blaming your middle school for puberty.

Perhaps your dip in spirits doesn't happen until later. This is unlikely to coincide with hikers' time in the Sierra because, simply put, it's people's favorite section[34]. It's also relatively brief[35]. The sheer beauty is likely to send weary spirits sky-high, making it feel as if it's the first day on trail all over again. As a result, this gloom may not rear its head until after departing the High Sierra. Making your way into

---

[34] Mac. (2015, December 17). The Annual Pacific Crest Trail Thru-Hiker Survey (2015). Retrieved January 18, 2016, from http://www.halfwayanywhere.com/trails/pacific-crest-trail/pacific-crest-trail-hiker-survey-2015/

[35] Perhaps the only period in your life where moving a few hundred miles on foot could seem "brief".

Northern California, you notice your drive beginning to diminish. The daily fire is gone and a dull sense of routine takes its place. The same sense of tedium you were escaping in your *prior* life. What is going on?

To clarify, the trail doesn't actually become less exciting. Sure, some days will yield better views than others, but you're still *living outside*. You're still traveling across the country on foot. What's happening is that you're adapting to your new lifestyle. Sleeping in a tent is the new normal and sleeping in a bed is what stands out as weird. This new daily routine loses its novelty, *it's just what you do*

Many interpret this feeling of lowered spirits as their cue to vacate the trail. "This just isn't as fun as it was a few weeks ago, I can only imagine how it will be in a few months from now." Letting yourself fall into a trap is a huge mistake. *If you bail out each time a honeymoon period ends, you won't ever follow through with any worthwhile challenge in life.* Relationships get harder. The enthusiasm for a new job fades. The new diet loses its appeal. For the first time, you notice the red "eject" button in your periphery. Your hand hovers atop, trembling, waiting for the last straw to fall. You begin to focus on the negatives, and seek the *next Pacific Crest Trail* to pull you out of your rut.

How Can You Avoid the Death of the Honeymoon?

The best defense against the lull that happens at the end of honeymoon phase is *to expect it*. By reading this far into the chapter, you've done ninety percent of the work.

I'm a bit anal about the mental preparation required for major life events (hence this book). I have an unhealthy obsession with needing to know what to expect. It's my coping mechanism. Although you can't predict everything that will be thrown your way, nor should you try, previous setbacks certainly help to prepare for each successive setback. I had already been through many major lifestyle changes in my life- studying abroad, going to a school where I knew no one (University of Wisconsin-Madison), moving across the country to a city where I knew no one (San Diego), and being part of my share of "failed" relationships; I went into my thru-hike overqualified for the position of "Chief of Mini-Crisis Management".

That doesn't mean you should sit around waiting for the trail to stop being fun – *that won't happen.* You're living outside. That's fun (source: common sense)! But, as I've stated already, it eventually becomes incrementally less fun. Don't blame the trail. Don't blame repetitive scenery. Blame human nature.

If, or more likely, when, the death of the honeymoon strikes you, take that as your cue to go back to your lists about the reasons you're hiking the PCT. For me, when the luster faded, I found it tremendously helpful to think about what my alternative would be: seventy-hour workweeks, undue stress, and the realization that my decompression time would likely be spent on a long hike. Perspective was quickly regained, my smile returned, and the temporary cloud of routine lifted. Your lists will help you realize this as well.

Or perhaps once the trail starts to feel routine, change your routine. Take side trails to waterfalls. Take a vacation from your vacation by meeting up with friends for a couple days off trail. Buy a few new audiobooks to occupy your attention for a few hours out of the day.

The key takeaway is that the act of expecting this honeymoon period to fade may be enough to douse its flames (or keep it at bay). At the very least, hopefully you now realize that this phase isn't reason enough to abandon your adventure.

Chapter 5 - Hike Your Own Hike

I f there is one single motto that pervades the culture of thru-hiking, it is the title of this chapter – *Hike Your Own Hike*. Although I had heard this maxim before embarking on the trail, it seemed cliché and hollow. I'm guessing there's a pretty good chance this phrase is at least somewhat meaningless to you as well. What exactly does "hiking your own hike" mean? You're the one taking more than five million steps, the hike belongs to you. It is *your* hike.

But there's a deeper meaning to this phrase. During your hike, you will come to several forks in the road (both literally and figuratively), and only you will know which is the correct route (this time only in the figurative sense). These divergences will surface in the form of group dynamics, the *proper* approach to thru-hiking, and the use of technology- just to highlight a few. This chapter will help you understand some of the choices you will be confronted with as well as the considerations to weigh before heading down one path versus another.

Social Dynamics on the Pacific Crest Trail

First Day of Class

*The following section applies mostly to NOBO thru-hikers
leaving on or around the Annual Day Zero Pacific Crest Trail
Kick Off (ADZPCTKO). Those who hike north-bound beginning
in mid-April to early May accounts for the largest portion of
PCT thru-hikers[36]. Nevertheless, the basic principles in this
section apply to all thru-hikers.*

During the first week or two, the trail feels similar to
your first day of school. Since many people venture onto the
PCT by themselves[36], the majority of folks are eager to make
new friends. Even a spirit independent enough to embark
on a 2,650 mile hike by his/her lonesome is eager to find
companionship once they step foot onto the trail. Being
thrust into such a radically different lifestyle can leave you
feeling a bit unsettled. The only stimulus that reminds you
of your former life is that of a fellow human being (and
beer). Additionally, knowing that there are others going
through the same set of emotions allows you to quickly
build a tight bond.

You will also come to find that many people are hiking
the trail for the same or similar reasons you are. They just
graduated, hate their jobs, they've hit a lull in their lives
and are craving some adventure, their friend did it a few
years ago and his or her thru-hike has inspired their own,
they're recently retired or divorced, has been sitting idly on
their bucket list, and so on. These commonalities only serve
to enhance the early stage *love-aplooza*. If nothing else, you
and the person next to you have at least one thing in
common: you're both batshit crazy![37]

It is for these reasons that group sizes tend to be
largest in the beginning. You will see massive groups of
hikers at the same water source early on. When arriving to
town, it'll be impossible *not* to run into other thru-hikers.
This may not be the case later in the hike, but in the
beginning, *this is the norm.*

---

[36] Mac. (2015, December 17). The Annual Pacific Crest Trail Thru-
Hiker Survey (2015). Retrieved January 18, 2016, from
http://www.halfwayanywhere.com/trails/pacific-crest-trail/pacific-
crest-trail-hiker-survey-2015/

[37] As defined by living outside for a half year seeming like a good
idea.

Reality Begins to Set In

Anywhere from the first few days to the first few weeks you start to realize that perhaps you have less in common with your hiking partners than you originally thought. A prim and proper 4th grade school teacher and 19-year-old pothead just aren't as compatible as they may have originally thought. The person you're hiking with thinks he or she is the funniest person west of the Mississippi, you feel otherwise. Or maybe you and your hiking partner are similar on paper, but for whatever reason, hiking together feels like mixing oil and water. As nerves begin to settle, your criteria for companionship begins to grow more refined. The grouping by proximity model starts to unravel.

Soon, you'll start to consider a new criterion for camaraderie: hiking pace. In these early stages groups are still in constant flux. Since there are enough people around, you can move at whatever pace best suits you and not have to fear ending the day several miles away from the closest person. You may go through three groups in a week. One group wants to press on but your legs are screaming fatigue. Another group wants to call it a day but you are still teeming with energy. Knowing that the next campsite will likely have fellow thru-hikers leaves you feeling comfortable enough to do as you please. There's reassurance in knowing there will be company up ahead.

A Few Weeks Later

On the whole, groups seem to become more stable, but injury and illness now shape a group's composition. One person in your group comes down with nagging shin splints and needs to take a couple days off. Another person drank some bad water and is a slave to the toilet for the remainder of the week. Yet another needs to get off trail for a few days to attend their best friend's wedding. Although you feel badly and will miss their companionship, you didn't budget extra days off this early in the trail. So, before you know it, the mini-parade you were marching in before is now down to a just a handful of people, or less.

What you lose in quantity, you make up for in quality many times over. You build very tight bonds in a relatively short period of time. Living outside has a tendency to strip a person down to their purest essence. There is no personality masking. This, in combination with spending several hours together every day, chatting over snack breaks, staking up your tent next to one another, and piling multiple bodies into a small two bed motel room, has a way of speeding up the bonding process. At no other time in life will you feel more comfortable repeatedly farting in front of someone you've known for less than a month.

This smaller group dynamic remains intact for a significant period of time. For some, this may last for the remainder of the trail. For most, however, they get to a point where the trail no longer causes any sort of unsettled nerves. They've been living in the backcountry for a while, and they're truly starting to feel at home. It is at this point where the motto "hike your own hike" will begin to resonate.

Hiking Your Own Hike

There may very likely come a day where you feel at odds with your group or partner. It may not be the result of direct conflict, although it may very well be (we'll get into that in a minute). Perhaps they want to spend the day on the porch of a general store eating corn dogs, and you want to hike out. Maybe they want to do an eight-mile day into the next town and you want to push further. Or perhaps you don't want to stay in a motel because you're going through your budget faster than you had anticipated. Up until this point, you would concede to the group's needs for the sake of your emotional comfort, but your last couple of compromises left you second-guessing yourself. You knew they weren't in your best interests. By now, you've hit your "hiker stride" and have a new sense of calm on the trail, you don't require the company of others. You begin to wonder, "*What if?*"

As strange as it sounds, thru-hiking is a "selfish" experience. You're taking time off to do something for yourself. Although this term carries a negative connotation, in this instance, I use the phrase exclusively positively. In taking on the Pacific Crest Trail you will ultimately become a more confident, happier person. You will gain a clearer perspective of what matters in your life. Ultimately, when you feel happier and more confident, you are better able to serve others. In this instance, selfishness begets selflessness.

Some lose sight of this once they get on the trail and get into a comfortable routine. The do-as-the-group-does mentality may very well stunt their individual growth. They're afraid to break loose, not because they fear going it alone or because they think sticking together is in their best interest, but because they don't want to hurt the feelings of people with whom they've formed close bonds.

This concern is unnecessary; leaving one's group won't be taken personally. Most hikers know that people hike the trail for a variety of reasons- to chase adventure, accomplish a monumental feat, and/or to find themselves. For many people, going it alone is the only way to fulfill these desires; they simply can't achieve these moments of profound introspection without solitude. Your group will understand this. In fact, your courage may very well be the catalyst for others venturing out on their own.

"I love to be alone. I never found the companion that was so companionable as solitude"

– Henry David Thoreau

Butting Heads

It's not unheard of to hit a breaking point with a person or people in your group. Have you ever spent five months straight with the same individual? One day together can feel like a long time. A half-year feels like three-fourths of an eternity[38]. A significant percent of marriages end in

---

[38] That's math.

divorce. Hopefully, more thought and energy is put into the selection of one's spouse than one's hiking partner(s).

When a breaking point occurs, you will have to choose between what's familiar and what's best for you. For most, this red flag marks the beginning of their need for independence; their own personal journey within a journey. This is the point where hikers learn who they are at their core; they to get see how they react to situations where there isn't the crutch of someone else making the decisions, or at the very least, providing input. This is where confidence is gained. Most importantly, when there's no one around to talk to or confer with, a calmness and increased level of awareness take over your mind. Instead of being the passenger in your car, you are now behind the wheel, and you become fully attentive.

Some people never leave their group, even if they've grown rather frustrated with their hiking partners. I witnessed this in more than one of the groups around me on the Appalachian Trail. Toward the tail end of the trail, a fellow hiker hit a boiling point with a couple of the guys in his group. He felt there was a gap in ethics and that some of the guys were disrespectful. Although he never liked their less than respectful actions, he put up with them. He was reluctant to voice his opinion with others, but he eventually confided in me. By this time, however, the hike was almost over. "I'm worried that I will look back at this experience and wish that I had spent more time by myself," he told me.

Don't leave the trail with regrets. Do what's best for you. Hike your own hike.

Alone, together

Although I refer to hiking the trail "alone," this is not exactly an accurate description. Odds are, you will rarely go a significant period without running into other thru-hikers. You may find that you end up with these hikers at the same campsite every night for a week straight. Perhaps you move faster than this particular group/person but you take more breaks. This can happen with a person, group, or several groups. It begins to feel like a carousel of familiar hiker faces. When it comes time to go into town and split a motel room, there is almost always a friendly hiker nearby to join you. The following day, you and your roommate might end up at different campsites, but again, you run into other familiar faces.

You will find that many others hike alone, together. You're doing your own thing much of the time, but you can still enjoy each other's company when you do cross paths. Much like the beginning of the trail, you will hike with someone for a day or two, and separate, only to meet up again as if you've never been apart.

The Story of Tee "Jambo" Corley

If the above doesn't convince you to hike your own hike, perhaps the story of Tee "Jambo" Corley will. After an unsuccessful attempt at thru-hiking the AT in 2011,[39] she took to the PCT in 2014 looking for redemption. Tee confessed that the dynamics of her group presented the most challenging aspect of her PCT thru-hike. I wanted to know what went wrong. Here's the story in her words:

"Jambo. Jambo. Yo, Jambo."

"YUP." I croaked.

"It's 5."

I unzipped the grey veil above my head and peeked out of my sleeping bag. Horizontal lines of boiling red and orange, deep purple and blue, tested my eyes. I gazed over the empty desert floor.

"Where are Lionheart and Slack?"

"They must have left in the middle of the night."

---

[39] Not only did Tee complete her goal of thru-hiking the PCT in 2014, but she got redemption by thru-hiking the AT in 2015. Tee is a badass. You can read all about her journey at http://bit.ly/teecorley.

The plan was to all wake up at 5, an already ungodly hour. Spirit Fingers was stuffing the last of his belongings into his pack.

"Well, shit, man. If we're not going to hike together, I'm going back to sleep."

This was one of many markers on my way to the slow and painful realization that none of the people I flew out to San Diego with, who I've known for years, who have known each other for years, were hiking the same hike.

Group hiking offers a sense of security and safety. I'm not talking about safety from the weirdo with the JanSport backpack, jeans and cast iron frying pan. I'm talking about the comfort of seeing your buddies' shining faces at the end of the day, having trustworthy folks to share a motel room, sharing 2,000 miles of adventurous life.

But what happens when you're too tired to reflect their shine, or your buddy is too broke to go to town, or yours are the only feet in the group that look like they have raw bacon fat just barely attached to them?

We never discussed what a thru hike was. We were all experienced backpackers, after all. We all shared one expectation: that our expectations were the same. We were wrong.

My group lost Lionheart a mere 77 miles in when we discovered he didn't have the money or the desire to stop into towns. He was also much faster than me, and I was struck with guilt when Spirit Fingers and Slack held back for my sake.

Not too long after, Slack, Spirit Fingers and I took a wild side trip to Los Angeles. It was novel at the time, but about 700 miles later, Slack decided he wanted to visit San Francisco for a week as well.

Spirit Fingers and I pressed on.

Finally, the group - meaning I - lost Spirit Fingers when we simply realized that our hiking styles were too different. It was unfair of me to make him wait at the end of each day because I wanted to take midday siestas...every day.

The dissolution of our group broke my heart, but it also forced me to acknowledge that I too had an ideal hike. I knew I didn't want to go fast, visit distant cities, or skip out on towns entirely. So, what did I want? I wanted to keep a continuous footpath from Mexico to Canada. I wanted to visit towns and meet locals. I wanted to hike at a slow and steady pace to keep my feet from becoming two-buck chuck and my siestas from feeling rushed. Amazingly, I met a hiking partner who happened to share these notions of an ideal thru hike.

By Northern California, my group had gone. I was hiking with Apple Butter when we were confronted with an onerous obstacle. Wildfires had closed off the Trail in a couple 20-mile sections. Hikers all around us were hitching up to Ashland, Oregon. I was torn. I'd walked through nearly the whole state of California – quite a large state! I was passionate about maintaining my goal of keeping a continuous footpath, but safety comes first. It was time to weigh our options. Apple Butter and I found every map of every Forest Service road, alternate trail options, and the most recent maps of the fires. We talked to the firefighters and forest service staff about various routes and the nature of fire, then we made a plan. We hiked logging roads a safe distance around the fires, adding innumerable miles and agonizing days to our hike. But I'll be damned if we didn't walk into Oregon.

This insane dedication to my hike and to myself impressed Slack and Spirit Fingers so much that they waited for me. My amazing friends actually waited for me. They hiked slow days, leaving me notes with treasure maps to hidden beers that filled my stomach and my heart. I finally caught them just past Stehekin, Washington, and we crossed into Canada together. This golden moment in the strength of our friendship did not come from the burden of hiking together – it came from the beauty of hiking our own hikes.

Unexpected Solitude

As Jambo's story illustrates, hiking alone isn't always a decision. In the scenario you wind up by yourself *against your will*, it's in your best interest to have a plan of action. In other words, have a means for coping. We will cover some of these strategies in Chapter 7, but generally speaking, it's a good idea to be open to the idea of solo hiking *before* circumstances dictate it.

If, or more likely when, this happens, focus on the positives. This is an opportunity to improve your sense of independence. This is an opportunity to become even more present. This is an opportunity for growth. Maybe you are a social creature, but finding peace during periods of solitude is one of the most valuable skills a person can posses.

The prospect of hiking without a cohort may scare you now, but that will change once out on the trail. I wouldn't have taken on a thru-hike without a partner[40]. The idea of living in the woods absolutely terrified me, and doing this without the aid of a familiar face was out of the question.

---

[40] I see this quite frequently in my work with thru-hikers today as well. This is a mistake. As we said in the beginning of this chapter, you're bound to meet an abundance of interesting, fun, and like-minded people right off the bat. The important difference between these individuals and a potential pre-determined hiking partner is the expectation of hiking 2,650 miles together. One is marriage, the other is speed dating. If you're going to go the marriage route, you better be damned sure you enjoy each other's company in high-stress, close-proximity situations.

But it didn't take long before learning that I actually preferred to hike by myself. Within a few weeks, maybe less, you'll become comfortable with living outside and won't *need* the crutch of a familiar face person to sustain this comfort. Take my word for it.

The Takeaway

This chapter is not intended to be a lecture on why you should hike some or any of the Pacific Crest Trail by yourself. There are those who go onto the trail hoping to find new friends, their soulmates, and/or future husbands or wives, and accomplish exactly that. There are those who go onto the trail looking for no such thing but end up with many new lifelong relationships nonetheless. It happens more often than it doesn't.

By all means, if you find a group that you really bond with, that truly meshes with your personality, don't split for the sake of splitting. If you're all on the same page about hiking pace, financial expenditure, and trail etiquette, and you feel no desire to go it alone, keep on as is. *If it ain't broke, don't fix it.*

The point of this chapter is for you to keep in mind why you're hiking the PCT. In my observation, the majority of the people on the trail are independent spirits. I write this because I want you to remember that you need to do what's *best* for you, even if it's not the *easiest* option. There's a decent chance you'll never have another experience like this in your life. You don't want to leave with regrets. You don't want to leave wishing you had pushed yourself more. You don't want to finish thinking you didn't get as much out of your journey as possible. This path is going to look different for everyone, be sure it's your own.

Now that you have some insight into the social intricacies, you will need to consider another, perhaps even more fundamental, question.

What is a Thru-Hike?

This question is capable of sparking heated debate. On the surface, the answer seems straightforward enough: "to hike the entire Pacific Crest Trail in less than a year"[41]. But exactly *how* one hikes the trail is where disagreement originates. While there's no official definition of a thru-hike, there are a variety of thoughts on the matter.

At one end of the spectrum, a thru-hike is a continuous footpath, monument to monument- no exceptions. You must walk every single inch of the PCT. When you leave a campsite, you must get back on the trail exactly where you stepped off. Carly recalls a fellow hiker who hitched into town to resupply, was dropped off a few hundred feet ahead of where he was picked up, and walked back to the original pickup point to cover the missed ground. Some people are hardcore.

The other extreme says that thru-hiking is more a frame of mind. You're walking, you're hitching up the trail, you're spending a lot of time outdoors. It's quality over quantity. Some in this camp feel that it's less about *how* they hike and more about *who* they're hiking with. Consequently, they'll bypass sections of the trail to rejoin their trail family. For people who fall into this category, thru-hiking is a lifestyle, not a rigid athletic endeavor.

Most people fall somewhere in between. Try not to get caught up in the semantics of your hike. Sharing a footpath does not equate to sharing a definition. Ask yourself what a thru-hike means to you. If it means walking every inch of the PCT, retracing your steps by a few feet to have a continuous footpath, or just about spending more time than ever with nature, you're right. Do what lights you up. This is *your* experience.

One point of clarification on the above paragraph, hiking your own hike does not give you permission to violate the principles of Leave No Trace, which are highlighted at the end of this book. Similarly, under no circumstance should you hike a closed section of the trail. This is illegal and damages the trail, ecosystem, and/or

---

[41] This is conventional wisdom amongst the hiking community. The PCTA does not set a definition for what constitutes a thru-hike, presumably for many of the same reasons outlined in this chapter.

other peoples' experiences. It also wastes precious trail resources. For example, instead of fighting a wildfire, staff would be sent to enforce the laws against those who are hiking the closed trail, further exacerbating the problem.

Some may find it necessary to advocate their definition of a thru-hike[42]. Smile, nod, and change the subject. It's meaningless discourse that ultimately ends up at the same conclusion (hint, it's the title of this chapter).

Trail Closures and Alternates

Trail closures are extremely common on the PCT. It's all-but-guaranteed hiking a continuous footpath on the official trail in a given year *won't* be an option for you. Whether it's a wildfire, snowstorm, or other unforeseen event, being presented with an unexpected fork in the road is a question of *when*, not *if*[43].

Carly encountered this several times during her thru-hike. One such instance occurred near Crater Lake, widely regarded as one of the most beautiful stretches along PCT for it's stunning, deep blue color and surrounding cliffs[44]. While Carly huddled around the campfire with a dozen fellow hikers at Mazama Campground in Oregon, the group took turns sharing their excitement for the forthcoming section. Right on cue, another thru-hiker approached the campground to present the news that the section around Crater Lake, along with the following 40 miles, would be closed starting tomorrow due to wildfire[45].

The news caught much of the group off guard and consequently roused a flurry of emotions. One person insisted that they would hike the trail whether it closed or

---

[42] There's far less judgment about the merits of a person's thru-hike on the PCT as compared to the AT, although it still exists.

[43] You can view all closures on the PCT dating back to 2011 at http://www.pcta.org/discover-the-trail/trail-conditions-and-closures/tags/trail-closure/

[44] Fun fact: Crater Lake is the deepest lake in the US

[45] An interesting note about the debacle is that the official PCT doesn't go along Crater Lake. The trail that borders the lake is itself an alternate. Most thru-hikers end up taking this alternate instead of the official trail

not[46]. Another stated his intentions to hitchhike to the southern border of the closed section, hike south, and figure out the rest later. A few were so distraught they were planning on skipping the section altogether. Many others were at a total loss for what to do.

As fate would have it, the trail didn't end up closing until a few days after everyone in the group hiked past that section. Regardless, this news of the trail's upcoming closure put everyone's personal definition of a thru-hike to the test.

This closure scare at Crater Lake wasn't Carly's first or last experience with alternates.

In Southern California, the trail was closed to protect the endangered mountain yellow-legged frog. There were two alternate options. One was a road walk that connected to an alternate trail that eventually rejoined the PCT. The other was another alternate trail known to be steep, treacherous, and exposed. Some hikers took the road walk, some took the more treacherous alternate route, others made their own alternate and followed the road the entire day.

Later in Carly's hike, a significant portion of the PCT in Washington was closed due to wildfires. Some hikers skipped the section entirely, some planned to take the alternate road walk, until eventually that too closed. Some decided to say farewell to the trail altogether.

So, what should you do when there's a closure?

Only you hold the answer to this question. Some insist on a continuous footpath, others prioritize the experience and avoid placing rigid constraints on this. It's possible that what's important to you will change between now and when you're in the midst of your hike. Just be sure that you're living up to *your* expectation of this journey, and not anybody else's.

Technophobe or Technophant?

---

[46] As stated above, you should *never* hike a section of the trail that has been closed down.

Another point of contention comes from the use of electronics for the purpose of entertainment on a thru-hike. For some, the idea of technology on the trail is sacrilegious. From their point of view, the trail is a sacred technology-free zone and indulging in it completely defeats the purpose of being in wilderness. Even if the addition of music or an audiobook would help to make their hike a little bit easier, they opt for a more natural approach- listening to gentle breeze, the chirping of chipmunks, the rushing of the stream, or the *absence* of noise. They might look down upon a person who carries a Kindle, smartphone, MP3 player or other electronic device because he or she is relying on technology as a distraction. Those same hikers often carry a pair of books (roughly a full pound more than a Kindle – a significant amount of weight to a long distance backpacker).

I feel differently about this. Technology[47] is all over the trail. Technological advancements enable people to carry full-size tents that weigh only two pounds. You don't see anyone on the trail carrying a six-pound tent or sleeping under sticks, mud and leaves for the sake of protesting technology. In my opinion, the line seems to have been drawn somewhat arbitrarily. Today's backpackers can carry their lives on their backs, with three days worth of food and a few liters of water, and only be shouldering fifteen to twenty five pounds. Twenty years ago, this would have been impossible. Gear has gotten more waterproof, more breathable, more durable, all the while becoming lighter every year. If you were to show John Muir a modern day thru-hiker, he'd think he was watching a science-fiction movie on backpacking. So much of what is available to hikers these days would have been unfathomable just a few decades ago. *Technology* is to thank for this.

I spent a good amount of time listening to music and audiobooks on my iPhone during my thru-hike. I love audiobooks, but rarely have the time to listen to them. I realized before departing for the trail that free time would

---

[47] Technology defined: the making, usage, and knowledge of tools, machines, techniques, crafts, systems or methods of organization in order to solve a problem or perform a specific function.

be my only abundant supply, thus giving me a chance to finally catch up on all of the intriguing non-fiction audiobooks that had been stockpiling in my iTunes library over the years. Learning the finer details of evolution *while* hiking made each wild animal encounter all the more fascinating.

Similarly, listening to music didn't take me away from the trail – it enhanced my experience. Music is art. Adding the audible pleasure of my favorite albums to the incredible scenery I witnessed added a new layer of stimulation. More importantly, stimulation was added in the areas that lacked it. There are parts of the trail that are dull and/or repetitive. If an audiobook is the difference between sanity and insanity, in my opinion, that is a trade worth making.

Furthermore, although the trail does offer a unique opportunity to "unplug" from the techno-craze of our society, the ultimate goal of a thru-hiker is to both finish and *enjoy* the trail. Without the aid of music and the spiritual audiobooks I listened to during my thru-hike, I still would have *finished* the trail, but I truly believe I wouldn't have enjoyed the experience nearly as much as I did. And remember, that *is* our goal – not merely to complete the trail, but to *enjoy it.* For me, technology contributed to my enjoyment.

Again, this is just my take. I am in no way trying to convince you to listen to music, or use technology in anyway while on the trail. I respect the opinion of those who feel that technology compromises their experience, I just happen to feel differently about it. If you feel strongly that listening to an mp3 player while hiking cheapens your experience, your opinion is completely valid. Just realize that it is *your* opinion.[48]

The Takeaway

---

[48] If you are going to use technology for entertainment, just be sure to be respectful of others. Strolling into camp blaring the latest Beyonce jam from your smartphone speaker makes you an inconsiderate jackass.

Hiking the Pacific Crest Trail is a unique journey. Your experience will be unlike that of any other thru-hiker. It will be of utmost importance to keep this in mind when out on the trail. There will be those who will attempt to impose their visions of what a thru-hike should look like. They will try to pull you in one direction or another, but remember that you ultimately choose your own path.

Part of the PCT experience is finding yourself. At the very least it involves gaining a better understanding of who you are. This growth will be stunted if you allow someone else to affect your decisions on the trail. Their beliefs are right, for them. Yours are right for you. They will hike their hike. You need to *hike your own hike*.

CHAPTER 6 - WHEN SHIT HITS THE FAN

Pacific Crest Trail thru-hiker fact #1: *there will come a time during your thru-hike when shit hits the fan.* It's all but guaranteed. You will hit a mental roadblock. It will come paired with physical, environmental, and logistical obstacles. You will question why you're still doing what you're doing. You will struggle. You will be pushed. You will hit a new low.

Predictably, *this* is where many get pushed past their limits and vacate the trail. It simply gets too hard. They have beds, friends, family and warm meals waiting for them in their other life. Why put up with this primitive lifestyle that is full of hardship? It's not fun anymore. There is no way to deny this dark reality.

Here's proof.

Enter Mac.

Mac is the man behind halfwayanywhere.com, his blogging home during his 2013 PCT thru-hike[49]. Although Mac's thru-hike featured several scenarios that could've easily elicited a white flag, there was one story that stood out to

---

[49] The site has since grown into a great resource of Pacific Crest Trail stories, information, and advice, including a thorough annual survey of that year's class of PCT thru-hikers, which we reference throughout this book.

me in particular. It went down more than 900 miles into his journey, and this is how it unfolded:

"Mac's Infected Toe" by Mac

Shit.

I plop down onto a rock and wonder how in the world I'm going to make it through another two days of this.

It's still early enough to squeeze in some miles before the sun disappears behind California's mighty Sierra Nevada, but the throbbing epicenter of pain crowning my right foot has other plans.

The fact I've made it this far today is a miracle.

I've struggled with ingrown toenails (when a toenail grows into the surrounding skin) since I was young, but never was I plagued with one this intense. Not wanting to take off my shoe for fear that I will find a blood-soaked sock inside, I hobbled over to the edge of the nearby lake to prepare for my now daily inspection.

Relieved to find my sock's color unchanged, it's what I find inside my sock that sends my heart, stomach, and morale plummeting.

A crust of hardened blood and pus covers the nail, as fresh fluid is pumped out the sides with each aggressive and painful throb. Red and inflamed, the skin has become nearly indistinguishable from the mess around it as my nail dives deeply in the wrong direction.

I clean away what I can and plunge my foot into the frigid alpine lake.

As I wonder if it's possible for any harmful bacteria that may be lurking in this lake to infiltrate my newest vulnerability, I lay back on the shore and question what the hell I'm doing.

Walking the PCT from Mexico to Canada? Yeah, that sounded awesome when I was home researching; looking at everyone's beautiful photos, reading inspiring quotes about nature, repeatedly watching "Into The Wild" to get pumped up - nobody told me about all this awfulness I would be subjected to.

What am I doing out here if I'm not enjoying the trail? Am I doing this because I genuinely want to? Because I love the outdoors? Because I'm stubborn and don't want to quit? A stab of pain shoots up my leg and reminds me there are more pressing issues at hand.

This toe. This toe is seriously fucked.

The soaking continues until the cold forces me to make camp and retreat into my sleeping bag. Tonight's dinner of trail mix and candy bars reminds me again that this is not the glamorous thru-hiking sold off-trail.

I really hope I don't bleed all over the inside of my sleeping bag.

The next two misery-wrapped days are filled with hour-long miles and more horror-filled scenes of my toe's slow and seemingly deliberate mission to destroy itself.

Although I have plenty of food and wasn't planning on stopping until Tuolumne Meadows in Yosemite (another 36 miles), I know that if I want to save my toe, then I need to visit Mammoth Lakes.

I check into a motel and cheer myself in true thru-hiker fashion - with a six pack and a large pizza. For a couple of hours, life is good.

The next day I walk to the emergency room to show off my prize toe. The doctor informs me that my toe is badly infected and that it may require minor surgery to if it's to return to working order.

"After this surgery, would I be able to continue hiking?"

"You would have to stay off it for a week. Honestly, you shouldn't be hiking with your toe the way it is right now."

Not hiking is not an option, so we explore alternatives. I'm given a ten-day supply of antibiotics and told if my toe doesn't improve by Yosemite, then I need to catch the bus back to Mammoth for surgery.

Sounds fair. However, said antibiotics need to be taken every six hours. Now, in addition to constant and horrible pain during the day, I will also be disrupting my sleep cycle at night.

I just walked nine hundred miles. I have nothing left to prove to myself or anyone else. The last two months literally amounts to the greatest physical achievement of my entire life. Getting off-trail now is what gamblers would call quitting while you're ahead. It's what an intelligent person, or a person with a horribly infected toe, would do.

Returning to the trail, this time armed with supplies to clean and dress my wound, I again find myself wondering why I'm doing this.

As we warned in the intro, we're going to tell it like is- and sometimes it is a bloody, pus-filled sock housing an infected toe.

Sometimes it's a pain that dominates your *entire* foot- as was the case for Kristin McLane, better known as "Siren" on the trail. During Siren's 2015 PCT thru-hike, shit hit her fan more than 1,700 miles in. In her own words:

"Aching Into Ashland" by Kristin "Siren" McLane

Aches and pains appear and vanish regularly on a thru hike, so I usually don't get too concerned. Unfortunately, the pain that started in my left foot on the road walk into Seiad Valley was different. I hiked a painful 25 miles to the Oregon border the next day, and 24 miles to the road to Ashland the day after, moving so slowly I told my friends to go on ahead.

I took lots of ibuprofen, spent the day limping along, and set up camp at dusk, alone near the road. I hitched into Ashland in the morning and forced myself to get all my chores done, even though the pain was getting worse. I got my own motel room to rest in private and spent the day distracting myself with TV, trying to convince myself nothing was seriously wrong.

In the morning, the pain was still shooting through my foot when I put weight on it. Between looking up my symptoms and knowing of other hikers with the same issues, it seemed I had metatarsal stress fractures, a relatively common thru-hiking injury.

I didn't think one or two more zeros would do any good, so I figured I might as well keep going. My plan was to give it a few days until the next resupply and see if the pain got worse.

I hitched back to the trail in the afternoon with a large supply of ibuprofen. In the previous days, my limp worked itself out after a mile or two, and taking ibuprofen helped. This day, the limp and the pain persisted, despite taking as much ibuprofen as the label allowed and stopping for long breaks. To make it worse, my altered stride to protect that foot had started causing aches and pains in other parts of my legs and hips.

I camped alone that night and debated whether I was being incredibly stupid by continuing. Was I making it worse? Could I turn possible stress fractures into real fractures, or was the pain superficial enough that I could walk through it?

Some injuries are game changers and some injuries are game enders. I've experienced both.

I had a game-changing injury on my NOBO Appalachian Trail thru-hike two years prior, breaking my big toe in Vermont. I limped a few miles to the next forest road where a trail angel friend met me with cheeseburgers and a trip to the ER. After a couple days off, I learned how to walk in a post-op shoe on uneven trail, and ended up slackpacking for a week. By the time the hospital-provided shoe fell apart, I was okay enough to continue cautiously in my trail runners. The toe didn't fully heal until several months after I finished hiking, and it still hurts occasionally thanks to injury-induced arthritis.

The game-ending injury happened on my attempted Colorado Trail thru-hike the year before the PCT. I took a bad fall, breaking and spraining my ankle in an instant. I knew as soon as I went down that it was bad—the ankle bent way too far, it hurt to touch, and I rapidly lost any range of motion. Another hiker appeared and stopped immediately when he saw me sprawled in the middle of the trail. He splinted my ankle, and I got to a road crossing by literally taking piggybacks from another group of hikers.

I couldn't help but compare my current foot pain on the PCT to my past experiences. Could I work through it like on the Appalachian Trail (a game changer), or was this more like the Colorado Trail (a game ender)? A few friends caught up to me in the morning and their casual comments about my stress fractures made it more real. My heart sank.

I knew I needed to get off trail.

I am the type of person who likes to have a plan, and suddenly I had no plan- that was almost worse than the injury. Not only was I getting off trail with no idea of when I'd return, but I'd be losing the group that I had been hiking with for months. To make matters worse, my hopes of a continuous NOBO hike were quickly going out the window. I needed to complete the northern half of my remaining miles first, to beat Washington's winter weather, which meant I needed to skip ahead.

As I left the trail, I told my hiking partners that I'd see them again, but deep down, I wasn't sure if that was true.

Both Mac and Siren completed their thru-hikes[50].

Despite the above stories, not everyone's *Pacific Crest trial* will come in the form of foot pain.

Jason "Shadow" Evans was dealt an unexpected blow on the home front two weeks into his 2014 thru-hike, when his wife called to say she broke her leg playing soccer, and consequently was unable to work her summer job. Suddenly the family of four was without a sizable chunk of

---

[50] You can read Siren's full story at bit.ly/SirensStory. The snippet provided in this chapter is merely the tip of the iceberg. Siren's determination is an inspiration. Also be sure to check out her personal site at wayfarer.me.

expected income. Though he insisted on coming home, Jason's wife urged him to stay on the trail, telling him, "this is bigger than us now."[51] A couple months later, Jason got word that his son needed a heart surgery to correct an arrhythmia. Again Jason wanted to head home. Again his family encouraged him to stick out his goal. Shadow completed his thru-hike, but not without an enormous guilt associated with each swipe of his debit card along the way.

One 2015 thru-hiker, who wishes to remain anonymous, came to the realization in the midst of her journey that she needed a major change back home. "The time and distance gave me the perspective to realize my relationship wasn't working." She adds, "I had tons of conflicting emotions, and that more than anything was the hardest thing about the trail."

I, too, know firsthand the trail has a way of testing a person.

Google Giveth, Google Taketh Away

Two weeks before leaving for the AT, I had managed to score a phone interview with a company I dreamt of working for, for the better part of the previous decade – Google. *Perhaps you've heard of them?*

The image of me pacing back and forth in my bedroom while nervously answering the question, *"What I would do differently if I were CEO of Google,"*[52] still lives vividly in my memory. After hanging up the phone, I felt less than confident about my performance. I was two weeks away from living outdoors; I wasn't exactly in the right state of mind to talk business strategy, or so I rationalized.

I departed for the trail, two more weeks went by and still no response from Google. I had finally given up hope of hearing back. This was both a disappointment and a relief. I could now focus solely on hiking and not have to worry about trying to find the one spot in town where I could get enough signal to check my email.

---

[51] Jason was hiking for a charity and had raised a good sum of money from several donors.

[52] For the record, this is not the position I was applying for.

Of course, the same day I relinquished hope, I received an email from the recruiter saying that I had passed the phone interview and that Google wanted to fly me to their headquarters in Mountain View, CA for an interview.

HOT. DIGGITY. DAMN.

I exchanged e-mails with the recruiter for another three weeks while trying to coordinate when I could get to a town that offered shuttle service to a nearby airport. Most of the towns along the AT are no bigger than a few hundred people, not exactly mass-transit hubs. Furthermore, as you will learn, trying to predict when you'll arrive at a particular destination two hundred miles away is a guessing game, at best. Terrain, weather, and day-to-day energy levels are variables in constant flux.

This was no easy task. If it were any other company, I would have politely declined. *But this was Google.* I had no choice but to follow through.

I remembered that my friend from college, Mitch (yes, the same anti-Tony Robbins from Chapter 1), has a sister, Jill[53], who lived in the trail town, Damascus, VA. Because Jill wins the *"Greatest Person on Earth" Award*, she offered to drive me to the Tri-Cities airport in Tennessee, an hour away.

My brief trip to San Francisco was nothing shy of surreal. I had been living in the woods for over a month at this point. Other than my few hitches into town, I didn't move faster than four miles per hour. I was now driving a rental car around a city I had never been to, while mentally gearing myself up for the biggest interview of my life- for which I was *greatly* under-prepared. Because the only clothes in my possession were my trail garments, I met up with a college friend, Brandon, to borrow his suit. I drove back to the luxury hotel paid for by Google, and immediately passed out in my king size bed. *Score.*

I woke up after my first full night of sleep in a long time and dedicated the next couple of hours to catching up on

---

[53] Jill, along with her husband Terry, run the site atraillife.com which has a lot of useful information about hiking and nutrition.

all the major technology news I had missed over the previous five weeks. I showered, pounded a cup of coffee, and began my drive to "The Googleplex."[54]

As I shut the door to the rental car, I caught one final view of myself in the reflection of the car window. *"Homeless clown"* was the first thing that came to mind. To say that the suit I had borrowed fit awkwardly was putting it lightly. Brandon is 6'2". Badger is 5'11". I looked like an eight-year-old who had broken into his dad's closet to play dress up. Additionally, because my already extra-wide feet had flattened out an additional size while on the trail, there was a *zero percent chance* of my fitting into his shoes. I had no choice but to rock my bright blue trail runners into this interview. Add a month of fantastic ginger-beard growth, and you have correctly envisioned me – *the homeless clown.*

"Hi Google. This homeless clown would like a job please."

After checking in at the front desk and quickly sucking down my blueberry Odwalla smoothie[55], a very casually dressed guy in his early thirties strolled out and looked around the room. *"Zachary Davis?"* I stood up, shook his hand, and was escorted back to a large conference room overlooking a nicely landscaped grass lawn where many of the very intelligent looking Google employees retreat during breaks.

Four half-hour interviews flew by in an instant. *"Estimate how much ad revenue Gmail makes in the United States in a single day." "Tell me how much profit is made from the Droid App Store in a year." "How many auto-mechanics are there in this country?"* Huh? Math? No one said anything about math.

Some of my answers felt pretty good. Some were laughably bad. I walked out feeling like I had just finished a twelve round championship fight. I got back into my car and started driving back to the airport, trying to process

---

[54] Google's headquarters

[55] There was an entire mini-fridge stocked full of these expensive smoothies. On the house, of course. The thru-hiker in me wanted to guzzle a half dozen in the waiting room. Unfortunately, the prospective employee in me interfered.

what had just happened. Although a month in the woods had drastically calmed my nerves, the business portion of my brain must have been covered in Snickers residue. Bluntly put, I had calmly delivered unimpressive answers.

I returned to Damascus the very next day and got right back onto the trail. I had officially thrown in the towel regarding landing a job with Google. *"Now I can finally focus on my hike."* I was merely trying to ease the pain from what I anticipated to be bad news from the recruiter.

Three Weeks Later

I got an e-mail from the recruiter asking to give him a call the next time I was in town. I was in town. I called him back immediately.

> *"Zach, I just wanted to let you know that the feedback I received from this end was excellent. Congratulations – you have passed the face-to-face interview."*

I was in disbelief. No way was this happening. I was in the midst of the biggest adventure of my life, and just found out that I had all but received a job offer from the company I would gladly sell my soul to work for. My spirits settled softly somewhere in the stratosphere. "All we have to do is submit your application to the hiring committee and we'll finish the details from there," the recruiter added.

The next opportunity to get to a computer and complete the lengthy Google application wasn't until I arrived at the Holiday Inn in Daleville, VA, another couple hundred miles north of where I had received the good news. The computer I used was either one of the first fifteen machines ever built or it had contracted all known computer viruses. I could have finished the rest of the trail in the time it took to open Microsoft Word. Regardless, I gathered all the required pieces and sent my application to the recruiter.

Over the course of the next two weeks, my mind bounced between the trail and San Francisco, mostly favoring the latter. I was planning what borough of the city I wanted to live in, how to get my possessions across country and which of my friends I could coax to move out there with me. When it came up in conversation, I was quick to boast of the job waiting for me on the other end of the trail. I texted those closest to me and let them know where I was landing in October. What seemed like an impossibility was now my reality.

The next contact I received from Google was the following e-mail, from the recruiter:

"Apologies for my delay, I was in meetings all afternoon. I did hear back from the hiring committee earlier today and unfortunately, I don't have good news.

They did not approve your application and as a result, we are not able to make you a formal offer at present time.

I don't have any specific feedback, as they don't share this with us regarding hiring decisions. I know this can be frustrating and I'm happy to schedule a call for early next week if you would like to discuss in more detail."

I reread the email fifteen more times to make sure I wasn't misunderstanding something. I wasn't.

Wait...what!? I had passed both interview rounds, and *now* I'm getting turned down? This must be some sort of sick joke. To add insult to injury, I don't even know why I was being turned down (still to this day).

The entire interview process began prior to my leaving for my thru-hike. I got *that* news approximately half way through the trail. I had spent the first half of my hike grasping onto the slim hope that I had a job with Google waiting for me on the other end.

Now what?

I was devastated. I proceeded to isolate myself from everyone around me. I camped alone. I avoided conversations at all costs. I needed space to process the disappointment. This was easily the lowest I had felt since stepping foot on the trail.

And then it got worse.

From bad to worse

Within a week, I started to get severely debilitating headaches. I assumed that perhaps they were merely a result of the stress that I had just been through. I told myself to give it a week and the headaches would go away.

Three weeks later, not only had the headaches not dissipated, they were far worse. I went to the hospital in Harrisburg, PA, suspecting that I had contracted Lyme disease (my biggest fear going into the trail). The results came back negative. The doctor wasn't exactly sure what was causing the headaches, but because temperatures had been reaching into triple digits, she suspected dehydration was the cause. She told me to drink more water and sent me on my way.

Three weeks later, despite the increased fluid intake, the headaches persisted. Additionally, not only did my head throb, but I was experiencing blurred vision on occasion. My moods were inexplicably sour despite my finally coming to grips with the Google debacle.

I was reaching exhaustion several hours earlier than I was used to. Twelve mile hikes over flat ground felt equivalent to a twenty-four mile day through the more challenging Virginia terrain. "How could I be getting in worse shape?" It didn't make sense.

I knew I had to go back to the hospital. This time a family member picked me up and took me to the emergency care unit in White Plains, NY. Again, the test for Lyme disease came back negative (apparently, it can lie dormant in your system for quite some time before registering positively). I got a CT scan due to my fear that the tension and visual disturbances were the result of a brain tumor. Luckily, they weren't.

The doctor proceeded to run a series of other tests, including a screening for other tick bites and blood infections, all returning negative. Again, since the test results revealed nothing else, the doctor suggested that I was battling dehydration. He urged me to intake more sodium and drink an electrolyte supplement as regularly as possible.

I followed the doctor's orders to a "t." I carried a salt shaker, dumping a couple teaspoons in my mouth every hour or two, and had my very, very, very worried mother send an expensive electrolyte supplement as often as possible. For about a month, this seemed to cure my ills. Unfortunately, however, the headaches came back, albeit less frequently.

Upon finishing the trail, since I would no longer be hiking ten-hour days, I assumed the headaches would subside. I was wrong. In fact, the headaches got worse. The first two weeks after finishing my thru-hike, I was couch-ridden, subsisting on a diet of aspirin and misery.

It wasn't until one month after summiting where additional blood tests revealed that I had contracted West Nile virus. Apparently the neurological effects of WNV can be long lasting. I wasn't able to get a concise answer from any doctor as to how long I could expect to battle headaches.

My headaches persisted for more than a year after my thru-hike, ultimately forcing me to move back home with my parents.

Turmoil, From the Outside and In

There I was, still more than 1,000 miles from my intended destination, battling the biggest emotional let down of my life. Less than a week went by and I contracted West Nile Virus, a rare virus known to kill those with weakened immune systems. Injury was added to insult, literally.

As surprising as this might sound, I can say with 100% honesty; exactly zero part of me ever considered getting off the trail. Call it determination, call it stubbornness, call it stupidity; I set out to do something, and *damn it*, I wasn't getting off the trail until it was done.

As demonstrated by the stories of Mac, Siren, and Shadow, I'm not the only one who has endured extreme emotional and/or physical adversity in the course of a thru-hike. Perhaps we're all stubborn, stupid, and/or hyper-determined. I can't speak for the others, but I wasn't always this way. The success of my thru-hike was the result of a conscious effort to shift my frame of mind before leaving for the trail. I learned and applied strategies that enabled me to stay the course, both physically and emotionally.

In the next chapter, I will share these strategies and show you how you can prepare for when the shit will hit your fan.

Chapter 7 - Conquering Obstacles

As we learned in the previous chapter, I was dealt a pretty nasty hand during my thru-hike. While my case was on the extreme end, stories of thru-hikers confronting adversity are quite common. Although you shouldn't anticipate quite so much shit hitting your fan, know that encountering obstacles is a matter of *when*, not *if*. Coming to grips with this fact before you actually experience the roadblocks is a crucial component to persevering.

I mentioned more than once already, a surefire way to deal with the challenges that lie ahead is simply to anticipate them. For example, in *The Death of the Honeymoon* chapter, I reminded you to expect your love affair with the trail to eventually lessen. Although the emotional fallout from a honeymoon phase ending can be a real challenge for some, the obstacles addressed in this chapter are on a whole other level.

These challenges might manifest in the form of heat stroke, hypothermia, skin infection, Giardia, or other waterborne illness. It's suffering from stress fractures, shin splints, or having a layer of blisters cover the bottoms and sides of your feet. It's severe loneliness, homesickness, boredom, or finding out that your significant other has found someone else. It's finding out that your income source, for whatever reason, has gone dry. It's having your pack stolen from right under your nose. This challenge – is *your Pacific Crest trial.*

This is the point when the next wave of hikers decide they've had enough. They could endure the rain, cold, heat, and immense thirst. These are all elements of the trail they had anticipated. The sprained ankle, however, they were not prepared for. They tell their trail friends that they're going home to rest and will rejoin the trail in a couple of weeks. They don't return. The sprained ankle tested their resolve and they failed.

Many of those who don't throw in the towel here are the most stubborn, determined individuals on the planet. Although the trail is an ongoing struggle for them, in their eyes, they have two choices: get to Canada or die trying.

I don't want you to throw in the towel. I also don't want you to struggle excessively. So, how can you have your Ramen and eat it too?

Is Your Drive Driving You Crazy?

Having drive plays an important role in *finishing* the trail, but it does little in terms of *enjoyment.* The tactics outlined in the *Mentally Preparing* chapter are in place to help you craft this drive. You already know my mantra- I don't want you to finish the trail if it means you'll dread the process. Thru-hiking the Pacific Crest Trail is meant to be an enjoyable adventure. No one is paying you to do this. You're doing this for *you.* The reward is solely intrinsic.

That said, not every day on the trail will be fun. If approached correctly, however, you will be able to sport a smile on the days when you'd otherwise be drenched in despair. At the very least, you will be able to keep a positive outlook whereby you might otherwise fall victim to chronic negativity. Once the record in your head gets stuck on, *"this sucks"*, it's hard to get onto the next song. So, let's flip the album over onto its other side.

The following are mindsets that will help you keep a cool head in the face of turbulent times. They're what got me through a demolished ego and West Nile virus. These aren't intended to build drive (although this might very well be an unintended consequence). These tools offer a way to reframe your *obstacles* into *opportunities*. In addition, these outlooks are in place to help you avoid the most common pitfalls hikers fall into when presented with these more severe challenges.

The following frames of mind are not my thoughts exclusively; they represent a compilation of the best advice I've received from others who have endured similar journeys, including other thru-hikers, as well as self-help and spiritual readings. Some of these suggestions will resonate more than others. Some may overlap one another. Adopt what works; disregard what doesn't.

Five Mindsets for Unwavering Mental Endurance

1) If you try to beat the PCT, the PCT will beat you.

We are naturally competitive creatures. If you're in competition with another person, it is your goal to do everything within your power to try harder and outdo their efforts. When you do, you succeed. On the PCT, however, when dealt a tough day, week, or even month, gritting your teeth and hiking longer days or increasing your pace will have the opposite effect. Put bluntly, pushing harder in the face of struggle is how hikers burnout and ultimately fall off.

If your car's caution light goes on, the proper response is not to ignore the signal and slam the gas pedal to the floor. Similarly, if you're having a bad week and can feel your mind's caution light switch on, get your ass off trail at the next opportunity. This signal happens for a reason. Without proper maintenance, a hiker's trail vehicle (his/her mind) will eventually falter. There's no shame in taking a day or two off to get a breath of fresh air (figuratively speaking, of course).

Odds are, after a couple of days of greasy food, bad television, questionable motel carpet stains, and the confining feeling of too much time indoors (this will make more sense to you once on the trail), you'll soon remember why you embarked on this journey in the first place. Also, remember this is an ideal situation to consult your lists, as it will immediately bring you back to your pre-trail psyche.

For some, this reminder may occur after only a couple of hours. For others it may require a couple of days. Take as much time as you need to get yourself sorted out. If you have a bad week, take a few days off. In your nine-to-five world, your boss might not be so understanding.

Those who fight against this feeling (or ignore it altogether), are marking the beginning of their end. At best, they're suffocating any possibility for enjoyment.

Please repeat after me: *"If I try to beat the Pacific Crest Trail, the Pacific Crest Trail will beat me."*

Good.

I'm aware that there are those who don't have the luxury of taking as much time as they want in town. They're either running behind schedule or on a tight budget. If this is you, the next point will carry more weight.

2) Don't just roll with the punches, embrace the punches.

It was December 2008, my final semester at the University of Wisconsin-Madison. My first class of the day started at 7:40 a.m., roughly four hours earlier than my body naturally *turns on*. The day's high was *negative* eight degrees, and with wind chill, it was *at least* ten degrees colder than that. I begrudgingly walked to my Black Music and American Cultural History course (seriously). In front of a half-filled lecture hall, the first words out my professor's mouth were, "It's days like today you either embrace the weather, or go completely mad."

This is the sort of mentality we need to adopt.

To take the "Don't fight the PCT" point a bit further, instead of fighting against what the trail hands you, take the obstacles as they come. It's part of the experience. *Embrace the suck*, or go mad.

Keep in mind, what we term as a "challenge" is entirely subjective. There are no universal challenges per se. It's the meaning we ascribe to events that makes them good or bad, insurmountable challenges, or opportunities to grow our character. What we call "reality" is really just an interpretation of events based on prior life experiences.

So if reality is a byproduct of our perceptions, it's our job to rewire how we perceive tough times. We need to look at the glass as half full.

When hiking in the rain, for example, instead of wishing that it were a sunny day, make the most of what is given to you. Smile. Sing. Splash in puddles. If you find yourself missing friends and/or family, instead of spending time wishing you were with them, embrace your current situation. Focus on growing tighter bonds with those that are nearby. If you're by yourself, embrace the calmness seclusion offers. It's a rare circumstance that you can get quality alone time in a beautiful wilderness setting. There is profound wisdom to be gained in these situations. This will elude you if your energy is spent wishing you were spending time with others. Remember, the glass is half full. See the water, not the absence.

If you can't embrace what's happening, you should, at the very least, accept what's in front of you. Wishing that your day were anything other than what is, is the fastest path to dissatisfaction. It may sound overly simplistic, but there really is great power in acceptance. In finding peace with what is, you will notice a sudden weight lift from your shoulders and your struggle will dissipate.

3) It's a marathon, not a sprint.

More accurately put, it's like 101 marathons.

There may come a time where you feel a need to just *get through* a section. The problem with this is that in the world of long distance backpacking, "a section" can translate to five hundred miles or more. Hikers will pick up their pace and/or hike ungodly hours to get to a destination they've ascribed as their salvation. When this destination is *weeks* away, you're all but guaranteeing suffering for this entire period, which can be enough to make raising the white flag seem all too appealing. I was warned of this phenomenon before my thru-hike, and I still fell into the trap. I will explain more about this in the next chapter.

4) This too shall pass.

It's as cliché as it is profound.

We have a tendency to get lost in the content of the world around us. If one is suffering from muscle pain in his/her leg, there's a tendency to frame this as "I am in pain" instead of "there is pain in my leg." What's the difference?

Surprisingly, a lot. When we confuse our existence with the content that surrounds us, we lose the boundary that separates the two. We confuse the content for *who we are*. The pain is a personal attachment. *I* and *pain* are inseparable. Because this is the case, it's all that we can focus on. Subsequently its effect on us grows infinitely. Our attention lives in the pain, and the pain becomes the frame through which we seen the world.

There is a simple yet deeply transformative solution to this dilemma. Space.

By telling yourself that *this too shall pass* you can create this space. Here you are reminded that there's a gap between *what is happening* and *who you are*. You are reminded that, like everything else in life, the conditions are only temporary. You realize it's important not to lose yourself in the moment because the *only* constant is change.

Mosquito clouds, freezing mornings, and sweltering afternoons are all bound to happen on the PCT. This simple mantra can cease to make you the victim and instead make you a spectator. You will see the light at the end of the tunnel. Presence emerges and the conditions outside of your control are no longer a cause for struggle.

5) Challenges are opportunities for growth.

I could've just as easily called this section "Everything Happens For A Reason," but there is often a loss for *what* that reason might be. In my opinion, this frame of mind more clearly highlights the opportunity that can result from your obstacles. For me, this point was the single most important strategy in overcoming challenges. I want to emphasize this. This isn't a tactic only for enjoying yourself on the Pacific Crest Trail. This is a tactic for instilling a sense of invincibility against any obstacle.

I'm guessing you probably know people who possess a "woe is me," victim-like attitude toward their daily existence. No matter what's happening around them, they're only focused on what's going wrong. Regardless of their circumstances, life is out to get them. Because of this, they develop a defeatist attitude- "Why bother? It never seems to work out for me anyway." The interesting thing about these people is that they are 100% correct. Whatever mentality you adopt will eventually manifest itself.

Whether you think you can or can't, you're right.

– Henry Ford

As long as a man stands in his own way, everything seems to be in his way.

– Ralph Waldo Emerson

The PCT is chock full of challenges. It is up to you whether or not you use these to your advantage or disadvantage.

Walking through a lightning storm won't just better prepare you for the next lightning storm. Knowing you survived one unnerving situation will calm you the next time another arises. When you overcome an illness on the trail, it will make the next injury seem less severe. Each challenge you face on the trail better prepares you for the subsequent one.

Of even greater importance in becoming better equipped and more confident on the trail is the way in which it will benefit you *off* the trail. The lightning storms will help you keep your head in what would otherwise be perceived as a tense situation at work. Being injured or sick on the trail will give you more appreciation for your big, comfy bed, Nyquil, and On Demand television. Crushing through the Hat Creek Rim will obliterate your former standard of working through the pain. Rolling your ankle prior to a 1,500 ft. descent in a hailstorm will put your *bills* into perspective. Finding peace in times of solitude will remove loneliness from your lexicon.

Inevitably, completing a journey as monumental as a 2,650 mile backpacking trip will leave you feeling invincible. When you get through this, is there anything that can touch you? *Hint: no*, there's not. You'll leave the trail feeling like Alonzo Harris, Denzel Washington's character from the movie *Training Day*.

"King Kong ain't got shit on me!"

It is precisely these challenging moments that you will reference as a source of personal strength to rise above *any* obstacle in life. For me, all daily tasks, no matter how *serious* they may be, now pale in comparison to battling excruciating headaches, blurred vision, 100-degree temperatures, and a crushed ego. The little things that used to normally irk me: traffic, a negative interaction, suboptimal weather and so on, seem to have lost their ability to rattle me. At least I'm not dodging lightning.

Remember, the obstacles in front of you are there for a reason. This is your test. This is your opportunity for growth. Again, look back at your lists, and rediscover what it was that you wanted to get out of the trail in the first place. Is it possible that these challenges are granting you the opportunity to acquire these traits? Are you going to struggle against it? Can you look your obstacle in the eye and laugh? Can you inspire those around you with your unflappable mindset?

This might very well be the greatest challenge in your life. *What do you want to remember about the way you handled it?*

Again, I want to remind you that welcoming the trail's hurdles will help you accomplish the ultimate goal: to maximize enjoyment. You're going to be on the PCT for a long time, equip yourself with a mentality that favors joy over struggle. You'll thank yourself when all is said and done. This I promise you.

Presence, the greatest present of all

Sometimes a positive mindset is hard to maintain. After a tough day at work, a fight with a loved one, or other form of unexpected bad news, one's mind has a tendency to head into a dark place. You should all but expect unexpected bad news on the trail.

The methods mentioned previously in this chapter are frames of mind. I realize that it's difficult to get back into a good place without actively *doing* something to make this happen. If switching from a negative frame of mind to a positive one were as easy as reminding yourself that *challenges are opportunities,* world peace would have been achieved by now.

Sometimes *action* is required to remedy the negative body chemistry that comes from an unforeseen hardship. Some turn to drugs, alcohol, food, sex, and so on. Not only are these much harder to come by on the trail, but they can ultimately compound the issue(s) at hand. Some choose to talk their issues out with others, and while this can be beneficial, you also risk it backfiring if your confidantes are going through similar difficulties. You can sink further into a hole.

What are we left with? *Exercise*? You already do that, *a lot.*

For me, meditation was a cure-all.

There is no shortage of benefits from meditation, "Neuroscientists have found that [those who meditate] shift their brain activity to different areas of the cortex – brain waves in the stress – prone right frontal cortex move to the calmer left frontal cortex. This mental shift decreases the negative effects of stress, mild depression and anxiety.

There is also less activity in the amygdala, where the bra. processes fear."[56]

Additional claims of meditation's benefits include an enhanced immune system, cured headaches, increased energy, decreased muscle tension and more.

So what do I mean by meditation?

The American Psychological Association defines meditation as:

> *Meditation is used to describe practices that self-regulate the body and mind, thereby affecting mental events by engaging a specific attentional set.... regulation of attention is the central commonality across the many divergent methods.*

Even by this definition, it's clear that meditation has a variety of meanings, but a central component involves the "regulation of attention". In order to accomplish this, one needs to find a setting with limited distractions.

What better place void of distraction than in wilderness?

The following are meditation methods I've used while backpacking. They represent a variety of meditation/spiritual readings I've done over the years. It's in your best interest to research meditation literature for yourself, as I do not claim any expertise.[57]

In all, meditation sessions should take about thirty minutes to an hour. If you're having trouble harnessing your attention when first starting out, try shorter durations, maybe five to fifteen minutes. As is the case with anything else, the more you practice, the easier it becomes. In fact, many find that their early meditation sessions yield little to no benefit. Keep the faith, you will notice a difference sooner rather than later.

---

[56] Allen, C. (2003, April 01). The Benefits of Meditation. Retrieved January 15, 2016, from https://www.psychologytoday.com/articles/200304/the-benefits-meditation

[57] If you're going to pick up only one book, make it A NEW EARTH by Eckhart Tolle and reread it as many times required for it to click. I have both the book and the audiobook and still listen to the audiobook regularly.

sure you that I was horrible at meditating when
out (years ago). It's normal to get caught up in
on of your thoughts. Don't get discouraged
happens. Gently let go of the thought and pull
k into the meditation without getting down on
yourself.

1. **Find a quiet place** with comfortable seating (on a log
   or flat soft ground) at least 100 ft. off trail to avoid
   getting distracted by other hikers.
2. **Sit upright** to allow your lungs to expand and
   contract completely.
3. **Close your eyes and begin to breathe deeply.** Use
   a ratio of 1:4:2 for inhaling, holding your breath, and
   exhaling, respectively. For example, inhale for a
   count of four, hold your breath for a count of sixteen,
   and exhale for a count of eight. You can change the
   length of your breaths and exhalations as long as the
   ratio remains the same (e.g. 2:8:4). Do this repetition
   for five to ten minutes.[58]
4. **Begin body awareness meditation.** Gently move
   your attention away from your breath and into
   different areas of your body. Focus your attention on
   your toes, feet, ankles, knees, thighs, stomach,
   chest, shoulders, arms, hands, fingers, neck, face,
   and head. Let your attention move sporadically
   throughout your body. Your body will let you know
   where attention is needed.
5. **Begin positive intention meditation.** Take time to
   recount all of the things in your life for which you're
   grateful and or appreciative. Feel the love you receive
   from friends and family. Once you're in touch with
   these feelings of gratitude or love, practice the body
   awareness meditation exercise described above.
   Focus that energy in the places that have stored
   stress or tension.
6. **Slowly open your eyes and quietly observe your
   surroundings.** Observe without judgment. Focus
   your full attention on a minute detail of your

---

[58] For more breathing meditations and exercises, I highly
recommend looking into Dr. Andrew Weil's work.

environment: a branch, a rock, a leaf, an insect and so on.

You may vary the steps in this mediation or do any portion of it. I have used the above format on a fairly regular basis to clear my head. Play around with different techniques to see what works for you. Meditation such as this lightens the burden of the issues weighing on your mind. Sometimes they evaporate completely.

Typically, I meditated prior to lunch to avoid competing with the digestion of food. You want as much free energy as possible. If you're really hungry it might help to eat something small beforehand. Try not to overdo it, as blood will rush into your stomach, causing distractions. If the middle of the day doesn't work for you, practice meditation when you can to find a time that does work. If you find it easier to do it upon waking or right before you fall asleep, by all means, do that. There's no such thing as a bad time.

I also found it helpful to practice meditation *while* hiking. This requires a conscious shifting of focus out of your head and into your body and/or breath. While walking, spend ten minutes letting your attention wander to the strength of your legs. Then dedicate the next ten minutes to focusing only on the natural inhalation and exhalation of your breath. Spend another ten minutes observing your surroundings without any judgment or labels. Just perceive.

This can be an extremely effective way to short circuit a negative thought pattern, thus restoring joy to your day. Additionally, this is an easier meditation to work into your routine. You're already walking- now you can multitask. Finding time to break without eating or socializing requires much more motivation and self-control. Even if you practice this for only fifteen to twenty minutes a day, you will find that you feel more energized than you were prior to the movement-based meditation.

One final point – it's in your best interest to start practicing meditation *before* hitting the trail. This is true for two reasons. One, it will be helpful to have experience with meditation so you're not discouraged when you get lost in your thoughts while trying to meditate on the trail. Two, meditation is amazing. The best time to meditate is always *now*.

CHAPTER 8 - SPRINTING MARATHONS

I would hate to admit that I would change anything about my thru-hike. It was the best half-year of my life. Even the most trying times from my journey turned me into a better person. As much as it pains me to say, there is a section of the trail that I wish I would've approached differently.

In *Appalachian Trials*, I went into good depth about my struggles throughout New Hampshire and Maine, the AT's final two states I somehow convinced myself that once I hit the White Mountain National Forest (simply referred to as "the Whites") in New Hampshire, I was on the homestretch. On paper, it made sense: 1,800 miles down, only 400 to go. Eighty percent of the trail was behind me. With only twenty percent of the trail ahead, I'd be standing atop Katahdin before I knew it.

This was a profoundly dumb belief for multiple reasons.

First, although 400 miles doesn't seem like much when you've already hiked 1,800, 400 miles is still 400 miles. Unless you're traveling by jet or dragon, this is an incredibly long distance. Additionally, the Whites and southern Maine are by far the most challenging section of the Appalachian Trail. Not only did I set my sights on the finish line far too early, but I did so at the exact time where my daily mileage began to decrease considerably. Miles were harder to come by, my yardstick grew longer, and as a result, my lack of progress became a major source of frustration.

Additionally, by focusing on the finish line, I lost sight of what was around me. Although New Hampshire and Maine are more physically demanding, the views through this section are unparalleled, similar to the way many hikers feel about the Sierra or pretty much all of Washington on the PCT. The Whites are the first point on the AT where a NOBO thru-hiker walks consecutive miles above treeline. Maine continues offering stunning above-ridgeline views, paired with a challenging, raw, yet immensely rewarding terrain unlike anywhere else on the Appalachian Trail. Simply put, in terms of scenery, the AT saves the best for last.

Sadly, however, I was too preoccupied with finishing to appreciate this. I pushed myself day in and day out, leaving nothing in the tank by the time I was crawling into my tent at night. I woke up each morning exhausted, with sore muscles and joints, and a void where my excitement and determination once lived. This quickly began to take a toll on my emotional well-being.

Those who exercise regularly know full well that there are days where you simply drag through your workout. This is a result of overtraining. Overtraining not only negatively impacts your physical performance, but also your hormone levels, nervous system, immune system, and moods[59]. In a state of overtraining, a simple thirty-minute treadmill workout will seem to last for hours. This effect is magnified in the context of a thru-hike. A day's worth of climbing mountains will feel like a week, a week feels like a month, and so on.

This obsession with finishing not only disconnected me from my surroundings, but it destroyed my ability to remain present. For the first time during my entire thru-hike, I was fighting the trail. As you know by now, the trail always wins. This time was no exception. Thankfully, the

[59] Kreher, J. B., MD, & Schwartz, J. B., MD. (2012, January 31). Overtraining Syndrome. Retrieved February 02, 2016, from http://sph.sagepub.com/content/4/2/128.short

idea of quitting ninety percent of the way into my thru-hike seemed too ludicrous to entertain. However, because I was too wrapped up in my own head to appreciate the immense beauty that surrounded me, I cheapened my experience.

I was definitely not alone in this feeling. Although some thru-hikers waited a bit longer to grant themselves permission to feel as if they were on the homestretch, this premature declaration was undeniably a common theme. Those who *weren't* talking at length about their expected summit date a few weeks in advance were few and far between..

Sprinting Marathons on the Pacific Crest Trail

In talking with dozens of PCT thru-hikers, we learned that this phenomenon is alive and well on the PCT, although it's less likely to happen during the "last lap" of the trail. For some, it will[60]. This is due largely to the anticipation of being done. The desire to return to your normal life grows in intensity. The same way you anticipate a shower, warm meal, and cold beer as you near town, it's quite common for hikers to start anticipating reconnecting with friends and family, their big, soft bed, and many (although not all) of the modern luxuries they swore off during their hike. Ultimately, returning home will reveal its own set of struggles (which we will cover in the next chapter), but the *anticipation* is common.

Many cited the anxiety of getting through Washington before bad weather strikes as a reason to rush. As Slug, a 2015 thru-hiker, puts it, "It was difficult because for the first time because I felt like my finishing the trail was no longer in my hands. I was facing the reality that even though I had the guts to hike the rest of the trail, the

---

[60] The struggle here only seems to happen with only a minority of thru-hikers, but enough that it's worth mentioning. This will likely relate directly to how much you miss your "former life" (e.g. significant other, kids, a career you're passionate about, etc.).

weather could make it impossible." This feeling of racing the clock can instill an additional layer of uneasiness.

For the majority of PCT thru-hikers, however, the marathon sprinting mentality doesn't occur during the last chapter of their hike, as previously mentioned.

Most report that their greatest emotional turmoil occurred in the latter half of California. By the time a hiker hits Northern California, the novelty has worn thin (as we covered in Chapter 4) and the scenery leaves something to be desired, at least relative to what they had seen previously in the Sierra. Additionally, hiking through the same state for *months* can rouse a sense of discouragement. This was the case for 2015 thru-hiker, Jennifer Kercher:

"There was a lot of focus on Canada from Yosemite to partway through NorCal. It was August, and we were STILL in California. Everyone started doing the math to determine how many miles a day we'd have to do to finish by October. It was really intimidating." She continued, "Northern California is a lot like being in the desert again: it's hot, there are rattlesnakes, and there are long dry sections. While in Northern California, I thought a lot about the impending snow, and I how I might not get to hike Washington--I knew Washington was going to be beautiful. It almost felt like I was trading a hike through Washington for a hike through Northern California. That thought was terrible for my morale. It was terrible for everyone's morale...This is the section where I saw the most dropouts, and other hikers started skipping very large sections of trail. There was a lot of pressure to skip with them. I didn't, and, by Belden, basically everyone I met up to that point was gone because they either quit or skipped ahead."

And then for others, Oregon supplies their biggest psychological hurdle. This was the case for Carly:

"Southern Oregon is a section of the PCT known for its easier terrain and beauty. While there are definitely still climbs in Oregon, the hiking is generally a welcomed break from the mountains of Northern California. I had been looking forward to this state since before I even set foot on the trail.

But shortly after reaching Ashland, I found myself camping alone, calculating how many miles I had left until I reached Canada and how many more weeks I had of hiking. I had hiked around 1,700 miles and had roughly 900 remaining. I told myself I could hike big days and be done in three weeks max. As I cried eating my cold, rehydrated mac and cheese dinner, I told myself I was bored with Oregon, bored with the trail, that I had learned everything I could possibly want to learn from this experience. I told myself that it was time to move on to my next adventure. I told myself I was ready to be sitting in an office again, wearing something other than the same clothes I'd been wearing for the past few months.

In the days that followed, I woke early, wanting to meet my new timeline to finish. I kept telling myself I would be done soon, that I just had to keep putting in the hours and get through it. At one point I even looked up flights home on my phone, but the service was spotty and I knew it wasn't what I actually wanted."

Carly's preoccupation with finishing was so powerful that she convinced herself to cover 42 miles per day for 21 straight days. For those keeping score at home, that's insane[61]. She eventually backed off this torrid pace when she reconnected with her trail family, something that was important to her, but regardless, this stretch marked a low point in her journey.

Whether your focus is the finish line or simply the next a segment is irrelevant. Fixating on a distance 400 or 1,400 miles ahead is a formula for frustration. Remember from the previous chapter that attempting to beat the trail is how the trail beats you. Overexerting yourself in hopes of finishing any given section faster is the equivalent to sprinting a marathon. Odds are, you're going to break down both physically and mentally.

So what are you to do when the "I'm ready to be done with section," thought creeps into your head?

The ideal is to remain present; live in the now. When done successfully, time disappears and the stress related to the future disintegrates. Unfortunately, unless you're a zen

---

[61] Unless your name is Heather "Anish" Anderson, who holds the self-supported PCT speed record averaging more than 43-miles per day for the entire length of the trail.

master, it may be difficult to sustain this level of presence for an extended period of time. Now what?[62]

Mini-goals

The first step toward achieving any monumental goal is to state it- and more specifically, write it down. Whether it's writing a book, starting a business, or becoming president, setting a clear objective is vital. Once the end goal is established, breaking this down into bite-size, attainable mini-goals is of equal importance.

After finishing my thru-hike in 2011, I set the goal to write *Appalachian Trials*. Before sitting down to write the first chapter, I broke down the project into smaller, more manageable steps. First, I crafted the outline. Then I focused on completing one chapter- or sometimes even a section or paragraph at a time. Next I focused on editing, and so on. If I sat down in front of a blank Word document thinking "Okay, now just write a book," I would have had an emotional meltdown that would've made Chernobyl look like spilt milk. *Pacific Crest Trials* received this same treatment.

The goal of hiking across the country is no different. Your focus shouldn't be Canada, it's the next 100 miles, the next town, the next campsite, the next mile, or sometimes it'll be as simple as the next step.

Let's consider the feat of a forty-mile day on the PCT, which is not unheard of once a thru-hiker gets his or her "trail legs"[63]. Doing so requires somewhere in the range of thirteen to sixteen hours of walking. During the course of such a day, you endure sore muscles, stiff joints, and acute pain in your feet. When you do *finally* reach camp, after a few hours of night hiking, your energy level is somewhere between zero and *near-death*. The small nightly chores- setting up shelter, brushing your teeth, eating dinner, retrieving water- feel exponentially more taxing. Sleep is the

---

[62] Only a semi-intentional pun.

[63] After about a month or so, you will be in incredible backpacking shape. Fatigue takes much longer to set in. At this point, you have achieved your trail legs, a common phrase in the hiker community.

only thing on your mind. Laying in your bag, you feel a tremendous amount of gratitude just being off your feet. Before dozing off, you consult Halfmile's maps or Guthook's app. You crunch the numbers and realize you've only covered *one and a half percent* of the entire trail. Quite possibly the most physically exerting day of your life resulted in seemingly zero progress. *"Will I ever reach Canada?"* you ask yourself.

This is exactly the sort of mentality that can quickly sour a thru-hiker's morale. A day's worth of miles divided by 2,650 is an equation that will always yield unsatisfying results. If, instead, you look at your next resupply (i.e. the next chance for a cold beer and greasy burger!), which is only 100 miles out, then a forty mile day gets you 40% of the way to your destination. *That's progress.* Suddenly your effort doesn't seem so insignificant- you can drift into slumber with a very deserved sense of accomplishment.

Although this mentality is less ideal than remaining present, it won't derail your ability to maintain a positive outlook. Allowing yourself to see progress will safeguard you from feeling demoralized. If you're going to look at your watch, track seconds, not hours.

The struggle that results from focusing on the finish line or getting through an extended section is avoidable. I realize now that I failed because I had broken my own rules. *Learn from my mistake.*

I looked ahead. I tried to sprint a marathon. I tried to beat the Appalachian Trail. Not surprisingly, the Appalachian Trail beat me. Carly tried to beat the Pacific Crest Trail, and it beat her. Fortunately, neither of these defeats were significant enough to cause us to throw in the towel. Countless other hikers haven't been so lucky. Focusing on the destination comes at the expense of appreciating the journey. As you will learn for yourself, the journey is all that matters.

Make yourself the following promises:

1. **I will not look ahead.** As the remaining mileage draws closer to zero, this task may become increasingly more difficult. Maintain a ninja mindset;

stay strong. Canada will come, but don't look past what's in front of you; it deserves your full attention and appreciation. *Right now* is the only time you'll ever have, it should be a damn good time. If staying present becomes too difficult, focus on your mini-goals.

2. **I will not attempt to sprint a marathon.** Whether it's the desert, Northern California, Oregon, and/or Washington[64], there may come a time when you feel tempted to "get through" a section of the trail. Trust me, the payoff from doing so pales in comparison to the penalty you will pay for pushing yourself past your limits. Realize that the desire to get past a certain segment has less to do with the geography and more to do with what's going on inside your head. You're now equipped with a vast array of tools to help keep a healthy mindset during these challenging sections. Instead of pushing miles beyond your comfort level, employ these tactics. This doesn't mean you should abstain from hiking big miles if you seek the challenge, but don't do so solely for the purpose of escaping the bad days. They are faster than you. A few days in town will be far more effective for boosting your mood than rushing down the trail. As the old thru-hiking adage states - it's about the smiles, not the miles.

By making these promises, you will put yourself in the best position to finish the trail strong, both mentally and physically. Odds are, you're going to have a lot of eager fans on the other side of Canada, more than you might expect. They'll want to know about your adventure and it'll take energy to convey your experiences with the enthusiasm this story deserves. Leave some fuel in the reserve tank for this purpose.

---

[64] It's important to note that this mentality may rear its ugly head more than once.

SECTION THREE:
POST TRAIL

CHAPTER 9 – LIFE AFTER THE PACIFIC CREST TRAIL

C ongratulations! By this point you will have just completed what once seemed incomprehensible. You'll have backpacked from Mexico to Canada, a true lifetime achievement! You'll wear your thru-hike like a badge of honor for the rest of your life. Nothing nor no one can take that away from you. Others will look up to you as an inspiration. You set out to do something bold, and damn it, you'll have done exactly that! The next time you tell someone you're doing anything, they'll think twice before doubting you. You're as crazy as you are ambitious. You will now be introduced to others as "that guy/girl who backpacked 2,650 miles". Be prepared, you'll have a lot of questions to answer.

But of greatest importance, you will have proven to yourself that you are capable of *colossal* achievements. You will utilize this confidence to propel yourself onto monumental feats in all other facets of your life. There is no challenge too big for you to take on.

Unfortunately, you will have almost no time to take a break before the next challenge slaps you in the face. In fact, for some, this next challenge will be every bit as daunting as your cross-country trek. This challenge, unfortunately, will bring no accolades or heroic worship.

What I am referring to, of course, is your reintegration back into society.

On the trail, you will very likely develop a fresh, new perspective on life. Over the course of five months, you adapted to a radically different lifestyle. You gave up your modern luxuries, and simultaneously shed the layer of insanity that pervaded your life. Five months without the media circus, ubiquitous advertising, and menial daily drama has a way of shedding new light on your way of thinking about everything.

Your life will have been reduced to focusing on survival and finding joy in life's simple pleasures. Stress occurs only in situations when it's warranted: running through a hail storm, unexpectedly stumbling upon a rattlesnake, or conserving enough body heat through the night to avoid hypothermia. Now the concept of a deadline, *who* said *what* to *whom*, how many "likes" your post receives, and concern about physical appearances are totally irrelevant. You will have reached a purer, more natural state of existence.

Eventually, you'll be on a one-way flight back to your former world. *What will you do?*

The Adjustment

There's no easy way to put it, transitioning back to your previous environment sucks. Like many of life's challenges, the best medicine is time. But also, much like the obstacles mentioned throughout this book, knowing what to expect can help ease this tough transition.

To take this a step further, there will be stages you can expect to go through in your post-hike world. I will describe the stages of my own post-trail adjustment, as well as share the insight I've gathered from other thru-hikers.

Stage 1: Toto, We're Not in Kansas Anymore.

You've just finished something that you've poured your heart and soul into nearly every day for the better part of a half-year (and even longer than that when taking your preparation into account). Then all of a sudden, one day you wake up and you're done. There's no more Manning Park to walk toward. However, it'll still take a few days for you to even realize anything is askew. Physically, it'll merely feel as if you're taking a zero[65]; it's no different than your normal trail routine. Mentally, although you'll know that you've reached "the end," it won't yet sink in. "I'm done. *What does that even mean?*" you'll ask yourself.

It won't be until around day three or four that you will know you've landed on a new planet. Your former world was in the mountains. *What's the deal with all of these walls?* The biggest adjustment will be going from ten or more hours of activity a day to being relatively sedentary. The constant inhalation of fresh mountain air was invigorating beyond words. Now, all of a sudden, it's gone. Last week you were running on an endorphin high. Now it'll seem as if your happy-neurotransmitters are broken.

Stage 2: The Post-Pacific Roller Coaster.

You will vacillate between growing comfortable in your new life, and longing for the old. You'll see some of your old habits in a new light. The people and places you left behind feel different, and somehow exactly the same simultaneously. As you look around, little things will remind you of life on the trail. You'll daydream back to a place where you measured time by the position of the sun instead of the digital clock on your office desk. At the same time, you'll remind yourself that you were clamoring for this life at various points toward the end of the trail. In other words, expect to be confused- you'll be up, you'll be down. You won't be quite sure where you are or where you're going. Some days it will feel like you're lost, while others will feel as if the previous half year was merely a dream.

Stage 3: Getting Back on Track.

---

[65] Trail terminology for a day off.

Every day will start to get better. You'll begin to look back at the Pacific Crest Trail with a healthy nostalgia instead of an envious longing. The confidence that you acquired through your Pacific Crest trials and tribulations will begin to surface in other facets of your life. You'll start to develop momentum in a new direction, whether it's in planning your next adventure, your professional career, or becoming involved in a new relationship. You'll start to reach stable ground. The fog will lift.

Stage 4: In the Flow.

It is at this point that you will have started the next chapter of your life. You will now fully utilize the self-efficacy that comes from achieving something as monumental as backpacking the length of the country. You'll settle into a routine that works for you. As you look back at the trail with admiration and nostalgia, you will realize that the next adventure is simply a decision away. This will bestow you with a sense of freedom. You'll realize that life *really is* your oyster. Whatever you invest your time and energy into will come paired with a new vigor and uncompromised determination.

But it's in these early stages that former thru-hikers struggle most. Despite the euphoria that comes with monumental accomplishment, many hikers experience an inexplicable feeling of depression on the other side of the Canada. I was fortunate to have heard about this phenomenon long before completing my thru-hike. I want to share what I learned with you.

Advice from Miss Janet: Post Thru-Hike Depression

It was a warm summer day and a group of twenty plus hikers huddled around a large picnic table in the backyard of the Happy Hiker's Hostel, the last hostel AT hikers reach before entering into The Whites. The night's menu offered home-cooked meatloaf, grilled corn on the cob, mayonnaise laden pasta salad, coleslaw, homemade buns lathered with liberal amounts of butter and, of course, Miller High Life. Hungry hikers were shoveling plate after plate of delicious homemade fare directly into the deepest part of their throats. It was as if we unlearned the art of chewing; a week of consuming only Ramen noodles can do that to a person.

This particular homemade meal marked a special occasion. The hostel culture typically requires a hiker to fend for him/herself. The Happy Hiker Hostel is no exception. But on this evening, we were graced with the presence (and culinary skills) of Miss Janet.

Miss Janet is an AT celebrity. I remember my first week on the trail, a fellow hiker (with whom I had never conversed), approached me and excitedly said, "Did you hear that Miss Janet is hiking the trail this year?"

"Are you serious," I asked, *"Also, who is Miss Janet?"*

Apparently that was a dumb question (my forte). Having been featured in the popular AT documentary "Trail Angels", Miss Janet is a legend of the trail. She has been involved with helping thru-hikers for more than thirty-five years, helping more than 10,000 hikers in the process[66]. In competition with more than sixty others, Miss Janet's hostel in Erwin, Tennessee was regarded[67] as arguably the best hiker hostel on the entire Appalachian Trail. Some hostels are known for their cheap rates, some are known for the quality of their accommodations. Miss Janet's was known for, well, Miss Janet.

That's why when Miss Janet talks, hikers listen.

We were in the midst of devouring said meal when Miss Janet chimed in, "Hey y'all, I know you're enjoying your dinner, but I've got a couple of important points I want to get across to you."

Her first point was after we get off the trail, we should expect to get fat. We laughed and quickly nodded in agreement. For obvious reasons, our appetites resembled

---

[66] 10,000 is likely far too low of an estimation now; this number was taken during my interview with her back in 2011.

[67] In 2011, Miss Janet closed down her hostel.

that of a pregnant dinosaur. There was little doubt our eating extravaganzas would soon catch up to us.

The second issue elicited a change in her tone. As she grew a bit more somber, Miss Janet began to discuss what was a common post-trail scenario: *hiker depression*. It was at this point you could look around and see more than twenty contemplative faces as they took to heart Miss Janet's predictions. Apparently, she struck a chord. Others likely anticipated what Miss Janet offered, but her words made this premonition all the more real.

Although I had heard some word of post thru-hike depression during my stint on the trail, I was unsuccessful in finding any concrete information or advice online. Realizing that I had a rare opportunity to pick the brain of one of the most knowledgeable AT minds alive today, I asked Miss Janet if she would be willing to discuss this topic in more depth, and she obliged.

I had the fortune of videotaping our discussion. If you'd like to watch the full interview (and you should), please visit: zrdavis.com/2302

My takeaways from our conversation are as follows:

- **Eat Well**: I'll cover this issue in more depth later in the chapter, but one piece of advice I can offer you is to look into nutritional testing after the trail. Wellness FX (http://www.wellnessfx.com/; Starting at $78) is a leading provider of this type of testing. A Wellness FX blood panel will give an in-depth analysis of any nutritional deficiencies that you may have developed while on the trail. Wellness FX also offers consultations with licensed nutritionist for additional fee. By obtaining this information, you will get a better idea of which foods to introduce into your diet to reestablish proper nutritional balance.
- **Stay Active**: As I alluded to earlier in the chapter, the biggest adjustment from trail life to post-trail life is the change in your activity level. Part of the change in mood seems to stem from a change in body

chemistry. Exercise produces dopamine, serotonin, and norepinephrine- feel good neurotransmitters. It's possible that the feelings of depression stem from the drop in neurotransmitter levels. Although this theory is only speculative, exercise has been found to be effective against depression[68]. Therefore, I'm sticking with it. In general, making drastic changes in your life causes changes in how you think, feel and in your body's physiology. To suddenly and dramatically cut back on exercise, a drug, a relationship, or leaving a familiar and psychologically comforting setting can result in withdrawal symptoms. It's likely you'll be exhausted after finishing the trail, and therefore uninspired to do anything active. But keep in mind, even light exercise can help. Additionally, being outside assures adequate amounts of Vitamin D from sunlight exposure, which has been linked with the prevention of diabetes, autoimmune disorders, multiple sclerosis, heart disease, and mental illnesses, including depression.[69]

- **Stay Connected**: Keep in touch with those who you befriended along the trail[70]. Although other friends and family will be there for you upon your return, they simply can't relate to what you're going through and what you've gone through (unless they've embarked on a similar life-altering journey). The friends you gained during your journey on the PCT will be there to remind you that you're not going through this transition alone. By discussing what

---

[68] Craft, L. L., Ph.D., & Perna, F. M., Ed.D. (2004). The Benefits of Exercise. Retrieved December 11, 2015, from http://www.ncbi.nlm.nih.gov/pmc/articles/PMC474733/

[69] Vitamin D Evidence. (n.d.). Retrieved January 20, 2016, from http://www.mayoclinic.org/drugs-supplements/vitamin-d/evidence/hrb-20060400

[70] Many thru-hikers even move in with their hiking partners after the trail. "TrampOn", a 2015 PCT thru-hiker, is now living with a few members of her trail family, and she adds, ""living with other hikers helps with rent costs, staying active, staying connected, eating well and treating ourselves well too. We are able to find work, coexist and know when the other person needs a day outside."

going through with trail friends, your issues
el normalized, thus helping you get beyond this
rary low. They will be your best support.

Pacific Crest Trail

There is another reason I believe that this depression can
occur. For five months, you have literally been moving
toward one single goal. There was no question about what
you were going to do on a given day. The answer was clear-
walk toward Canada. You were working toward something
tangible. Although it may have felt like adding drops of
water in hopes of creating an ocean, you knew that
eventually you would obtain your goal. Finally, after several
months, you could see the finish line. All of that time and
effort had finally culminated in your prize.

Suddenly, the first day after the trail, there is no prize
to work towards. Much like a withdrawal of
neurotransmitters, you're experiencing a withdrawal of
purpose. This can be avoided.

Before getting off the trail, spend time thinking about
your next adventure. Some will interpret this as another
backpacking trip, or similar outdoor vagabond journey. It
can be this sort of adventure, but doesn't have to be.

For Carly and me, writing this book has been the
equivalent of our next thru-hike. The first day sitting in
front of keyboard felt like walking up to the southern
terminus. We knew there'd be many days of struggle,
headaches, and self-doubt. More importantly, however, we
knew this book would give us tremendous purpose and
excitement. If we just took one step at a time, before long,
we'd have *a freaking book* to show for all our hard work. If
that doesn't get you out of bed in the morning, what will?

What's *your* next Pacific Crest Trail? Dedicate some
time to really consider what inspires you. It shouldn't
matter how crazy the idea seems, nothing can be crazier
than walking from Mexico to Canada. You will have done
that. You will have proven to yourself and others that you
can do whatever you put your mind to. *Go do it.*

I realize that some people have trouble identifying what
that next journey should be. For me, I find meditation to be

a great resource for digging to the core of what I should be doing with my time. If you're having trouble finding something to feel passionate about, prior to meditating, set an intention of "Why am I here?" and meditate on that mantra. Don't struggle to find the answer, the answer will find you. Just be present enough to notice when it emerges.

If this doesn't help you find something inspirational enough to move toward, make a conscious effort to start learning new subjects. Order some new books from Amazon. Take a new class. Talk to those who inspire you and ask what new ventures they're getting involved in. Find out what's available on the World Wide Opportunities of Organic Farms website (www.wwoof.org) or Workaway.info (www.workaway.info). Watch fascinating TED Talks (www.ted.com). You will likely surprise yourself with how quickly you can unearth inspiration.

Post-Trail Weight Gain, An Inevitability?

I reached out to former thru-hikers after finishing the PCT asking about their post trail weight[71], and the feedback I got was rather interesting. Not only do a lot of hikers put on the weight they lost over the previous five months, many end up doing so twice as fast as they lost it. A good portion even tack on more weight than they originally lost.

I found this to be curious. A half-year of endurance exercise and junk food must do something to a person's system that creates this post-trail weight gain. If they're determined enough to bust their butt for a five months, poor self-control post-trail seems to be an unlikely explanation for why many lose the battle of the bulge.

I researched this subject to learn what those who were able to keep their weight down after the trail were doing differently. To my surprise, I was unable to find any relevant information on this topic.

---

[71] Found at http://bit.ly/PCTweight

Unsatisfied with making only slightly educated guesses as to why this occurs and what thru-hikers can do to prevent it, I reached out to Nathan Daley MD, MPH. Dr. Daley practices integrative preventive medicine and performance medicine at the Leonardi Institute (www.leonardiinstitute.com) in Colorado. I specifically wanted to know if the weight gain was an inevitable consequence of going from extreme endurance exercise back to a more moderate activity level.

There is good news: Dr. Daley doesn't believe that post-trail weight gain is inevitable. However, staying at a healthy weight will take some work.

The following tips are Dr. Daley's advice on what you can do to prevent post-trail weight gain:

7 Tips to Avoiding Post-Pacific Crest Trail Weight Gain

1) Prioritize low glycemic foods on the trail.

Low glycemic foods tend to have moderate to high fiber, fat, protein and water content. Non-starchy vegetables are the classic example, but these are not easily packed for hiking. Drying anything (fruit or vegetables) increases the glycemic index/load. When possible, reduce consumption of dried fruit, granola, crackers, candy bars and sweets when possible, and increase consumption of nuts, whole fruits and vegetables, and lean meat sources (jerky, etc.). You may even consider adding a fiber supplement (for example, a small pack of Metamucil). For hikers experienced in the local edible flora and fauna, harvesting some wild edible plants is a good way to consume low glycemic foods with fiber. Just be careful, many seemingly edible plants are poisonous.

It might be helpful to know that not *all* dried fruit is a problem. Dried apricots and dried apples have low glycemic measurements and are acceptable, but raisins have a high glycemic index and load and are not acceptable. Low glycemic bars made of nuts and dried fruit may be convenient to have on the trail as well. I recommend LARABAR and KIND bars. Additionally, studies show that low glycemic foods are the best for maintaining blood glucose and replacing glycogen stores in endurance athletes.

2) Prioritize protein while on the trail.

This will help prevent weight loss and will help keep satiety mechanisms in place (protein, fat, fiber all contribute to a sense of satiety).

3) Let your return to civilization also be an entry into a new lifestyle.

Commit to a new nutritional plan. Retain a diet focused on low glycemic foods (vegetables, meat, eggs). This keeps insulin levels low and prevents fat storage. Have this as your plan before even starting the PCT in order to avoid fantasizing about starchy comfort foods like bread, pizza, burgers, french fries, etc. while you are on the trail.

Hiking the PCT changes people, but then civilization changes them right back. By committing to a better lifestyle once back from the PCT, you remain in control and, in a way, your PCT journey never really ends.

4) Prioritize protein, lean meats (fish, chicken, buffalo, elk, etc.), and low glycemic vegetables upon return.

This allows lean muscle mass to return instead of body fat and satiety mechanisms can help control portion size. Some vegetarian options include quinoa, legumes, tempeh and tofu, just to name a few.

5) Continue being physically active at a high level.

By this, I do not mean maintaining a twenty to thirty mile a day regimen, but take a regular five mile hike, swim, walk, run, cycle, do yoga, and so on. It's fine, even recommended, to take some down time off after your thru-hike to let your body recover, but formulate a plan to stay active and fit in your post-trail life. Active recovery (even light exercise) is better than passive recovery (sitting). Taking light walks beginning the day after you return can help you recover faster. High intensity exercise (intervals, etc.) is best for keeping body fat low and building back lean mass, but should be done only after you've given your body ample rest.

6) Begin contemplating or planning your next adventure.

Start planning your next adventure to avoid the post-Pacific Crest Trail blues. Give yourself permission to start to dream. This will help you feel upbeat, which will help get you in the mood to start exercising again.

7) Useful post-trail supplements.

There are a lot of supplements you can introduce into your diet to help you regain a healthful nutritional balance including fiber (acacia, psyllium, arabinogalactan/larch tree, and glucomannan are all good options), probiotics (20+ billion CFUs of bifidobacterium and lactobacillus species), whey protein powder (Solgar Whey to Go- it is a non-contaminated brand-used to reach 70-110 grams of total protein a day depending upon body weight), and MCT oil (medium chain triglycerides; thermogenic fats which help maintain a high metabolism)[72].

An example of a day's diet under Dr. Daley's plan would look something like this:

---

[72] I've written an article on the few supplements I carry with me while backpacking. You can find that at: bit.ly/BackpackingSupplements

If you're unfamiliar with the principles of a low-glycemic diet, three books I highly recommend are: The South Beach Diet, The Paleo Diet, and The Four Hour Body. The first two are focused solely on diet, while The Four Hour Body covers a wide range of topics, including diet and exercise, but also sleep techniques, sex, and injury prevention. Quite honestly, there are a lot of fad diets that all tend to use the same central rule: eat real food with a focus on high protein and fiber.

Don't overlook the value of a healthy, well-balanced diet after getting off the trail. Eating nutritionally dense and low-glycemic foods will go a long way in improving your sense of well-being and to keep all those hard-earned pounds off.

Summary

The preceding tips are unlikely to entirely prevent the momentary low associated with finishing the Pacific Crest Trail. See your blues for what they are. You will have just finished something truly awesome. There is going to be a let down from anything of that magnitude. Remember, *this too shall pass*, and when it does, you will like what follows- a new and improved you.

END: YOUR NEW BEGINNING

I was less than ten days from my much-anticipated summiting of Mt. Katahdin. I had been hiking by myself for a couple of days, rarely crossing paths with others. That's why I was caught off guard when I saw a pack of seven NOBO hikers huddled together on the trail ahead. This wasn't a logical rest area. They stopped on the slope of a hill, in a location lacking scenery or any inviting seating. I slowed my pace and continued toward the group. I was listening to the new My Morning Jacket album for the ninety-fifth time when one of the hikers, *Drum Solo*, started walking slowly in my direction. *Drum Solo* is the type who always sees the good in life and for this reason, a smile is permanently affixed to his face- except in this instance. Something was askew. As I pulled out my white Apple earbuds, he said, "Dude, you're not going to believe this..." he hesitated, "there's a dead body ahead on the trail."

Fifty-one year old, Michael Guerette- trail name- *Open Mike*, was hiking south from Katahdin (part of his SOBO thru-hike), when he hit the ground on a moderately sloped downhill portion of the trail. A pair of hikers, *Squirrel* and *Bluegrass*, were close enough to hear his body make contact with the ground. Initially they thought it was a deer, but as they approached, they saw Open Mike's body lying motionless just off the trail. They called the police, and followed instructions to resuscitate him, to no avail. Squirrel and Bluegrass believed that he died upon impact, possibly before. Judging from the lack of color to his face, he was most certainly gone by the time I arrived.

The whole scene was surreal. The other hikers and I sat and waited by Michael Guerette's body for forty-five minutes so we could fill out witness reports when the local authorities arrived. In the meantime, we contemplated the weight of the situation. Most, myself included, sat there in silence, in disbelief. What do you say after something like that? *What can you say?* Others offered their theories as to what happened. A couple of hikers attempted to crack jokes. It was apparent that they did *not* find humor in the situation. *They were uncomfortable*; they didn't know how to handle themselves. Aside from bodies that had been embalmed for a funeral, none of us had seen a dead body before. Needless to say, we were all rattled, even those who wouldn't readily admit to it.

The next few hours were a blur. The vision of Open Mike's body consumed my thoughts. My mind entered into a different world. I kept thinking of how easily that could have been any one of us. If it was, in fact, a simple fall that caused Open Mike's death, then there was no good reason to think we weren't all susceptible to such a tragedy. I began to recall the times I had gotten my foot caught on a root while hiking a steep descent, only to have made a dumb luck recovery, allowing me to narrowly escape serious injury. I recalled the times when I had actually face planted into the ground, only to notice a large, jagged rock on either side of my head. Over the course of five million steps, even if you're 99.99% accurate, five hundred of those steps are going to be bad. Was Open Mike a victim of the .01%? I always wondered how NFL football players get back on the field and run into each other at one hundred miles per hour after watching one of their teammates get carried off the field on a stretcher. I was now confronted with an even more challenging scenario. It was here that I learned the answer; you do it because you *have to*, not because you *want to*.

I began to think about all of his family and friends. I was upset because I saw the body. I didn't even know the guy. I immediately felt worse when I thought about all of the people who just lost a loved one forever. *A world of sadness can spread in an instant.* This was the *only* thought on my mind for the next few miles.

Needless to say, I wasn't much in the mood for hiking.

It wasn't until four hours after originally seeing Open Mike's body that I gained some perspective.

Upon reaching the next shelter[73], I sat down and flipped through the trail log[74] to see if Open Mike had entered anything.

He had.

His last post was a detailed entry about how great it had been to encounter a family of hikers heading in the opposite direction. He talked in great depth about how fond he was of the youngsters in the group, and that he hoped that they really enjoyed the remainder of their hike. He said it was a great pleasure to make their acquaintance and that it made his day. And then there was his sign off....

"Today is a great day to be alive. – Open Mike"

Still to this day, this thought gives me goose bumps.

The takeaway

Although Open Mike's passing is undoubtedly a truly saddening story, I feel that we should all be so lucky as to go the way that he did: doing something he loved, lavishing unconditional kindness upon strangers, and being the recipient of love from countless others.

Which brings us back to my original point: thru-hiking is meant to be enjoyed. *All of life is meant to be enjoyed.* Open Mike was doing it right. The simple, routine interactions with others "made his day". For him, every day was a great day to be alive, even his last. We never know when our last day will be, but this is of secondary

---

[73] The AT is lined with more than 250 three-walled structures which serve as refuge for hikers, averaging out to approximately one shelter every 8 miles.

[74] Each shelter on the AT has at least one notebook for hikers to sign called a trail log. Most hikers include a short note, joke, and/or anecdote.

importance. It's what we're doing with our precious time on this planet that matters.

In order to make the most of every day, we need to take responsibility for what's in our control, and surrender to that which is not.

What's outside of our control? *The elements.* Storms will happen. Soreness will happen. Sweat-soaked clothes will happen.

What is within our control, however, is much more profound than any amount of precipitation, it's our perception. Life will supply you with all of the props for the play, but only you are able to write the script.

Open Mike was exposed to the same storms that ultimately send seven in ten hikers home on the AT. The difference between those who succeed, and those who do not, however, is the story they tell themselves in this process. By this standard Open Mike was successful.

You will soon learn for yourself that hiking the Pacific Crest Trail isn't about arriving at Canada. Reaching the northern terminus is a sweet bonus, a symbol of your accomplishment, and a fitting *finish* to a truly epic journey.

Hiking the Pacific Crest Trail is about each and every one of the 5.3 million steps along the way. *This is the single greatest takeaway you can leave the PCT with.* This mindset will not only ease your struggle, it will ultimately make your entire experience far more enriching.

Similarly, life isn't about achieving a certain income, "making it" to retirement, or buying a certain house. *Like the PCT, life is about each step along the way.* The lessons learned from the Pacific Crest Trail will bring this profound truth into focus.

Don't take a single moment for granted and, like Mike, live each day as if it were your last.

When you finish hiking the Pacific Crest Trail

I don't have any children[75], but I feel a fatherly pride in you. Carly feels the same[76]. Your finishing the trail is of sincere interest to us. When you picked up this book, we told you that we feel responsible for helping you accomplish your goal- becoming a successful thru-hiker. We take that commitment seriously.

When you do finish, please, let us brag about you! We want to know about your journey. We want to know what about this book worked for you. We want to know what didn't. We want to know your personal story. Please, email me and Carly all of your Pacific Crest trials and triumphs at theGoodBadger@gmail.com and carly.moree@gmail.com (respectively).

Additionally, be sure to send us your pictures from Canada (or Mexico, if you're hiking SOBO)! We want to see the success painted across your face. We will share your photo on a dedicated successful thru-hiker page (at http://bit.ly/thruhikers) to celebrate your triumph with the world!

From the bottom of our hearts, thank you for reading this book. We eagerly await being able to hear the story of *your* journey.

---

[75] That I know of.

[76] In the motherly sense, that is.

SECTION FOUR:
BONUS MATERIAL

CHAPTER 11 – ADAPTABILITY

[by Carle Moree]

I n the process of writing this book, Zach and I spent hours discussing the biggest differences between thru-hiking the Pacific Crest Trail and the Appalachian Trail. Although the terrain, weather, and gear needs present differences, the challenges are more similar than dissimilar. As it turns out, a half-year thru-hike on one side of the country has a good deal in common with a half-year thru-hike on the other side of the country, especially in the area that presents the greatest challenge: the mental component.

However, there *are* differences. One of the biggest is a hiker's gear needs, which Liz "Snorkel" Thomas will do wonderful job walking you through in the next chapter. Many of the others, quite frankly, aren't worth covering, as the goal of this book is to effectively prepare you for hiking the PCT, not inundate you with inconsequential details. There are plenty of other resources available where you can scratch that itch.

One element worth covering, however, is the PCT's demand for adaptability.

Being able to adapt on the Pacific Crest Trail is critical. It could very well be the deciding factor between your thru-hike being pleasurable or painful. Before you hike the PCT, you might hear that "there's no water in the desert", that "your appetite will decrease in the Sierra Nevada mountains" and that "the weather in Washington will be brutal".

Some of these predictions might prove to be true for you. Others might not. The weather along the PCT, especially over the last decade, has been consistently inconsistent. The important takeaway is that the PCT will test your ability to adapt across a range of categories.

As mentioned in previous chapters, the PCT has desert and mountains, waterless stretches and snow, extreme heat and extreme cold, and mild and volatile weather patterns. Perhaps you've hiked through many, if not all, of these conditions. It is unlikely, however, you've hiked this variety of terrain and weather in such close proximity to one another.

Simply *being aware* of the necessity to be able to flow with all of these elements will make a tremendous difference during your thru-hike. *Expecting* punches and *accepting* that you'll need to roll with them will tremendously help your attitude when the unexpected does occur. Being mindful of these hurdles beforehand will help to lessen their impact. They make knock you down, but they won't knock you out.

So, how does adaptability come into play on the PCT?

The Lack of Water

For 700 miles of the PCT, water will consume most of your thoughts. From the Mexico / California border to Kennedy Meadows South, you will regularly ask yourself, "How much water should I carry for the next stretch?" and "Will the next water source even have water?"

The lack of water in the desert will be a major obstacle, especially in the beginning. You'll encounter seven stretches of more than 20 miles without water in the first section of your hike, the first of which will be your very first day - from the Mexico / California border to Lake Morena[77]. Then

---

[77] Data provided by Ryan "Guthook" Linn pulled from his PCT App. This is evaluating only "reliable" water sources and does not include towns- which are reliable but not always in the cards- or water caches-

there's the notorious Mount San Jacinto, where you'll lose approximately 8,000 feet in elevation over mostly exposed terrain for nearly 20 miles without water. There's even a potential 40-mile dry section, mentioned in Chapter 3, from Landers Meadow to Walker Pass Campground. I could go on.

Fortunately, there's a report maintained by volunteers that contains the status of water sources. The PCT Water Report can be found online at: http://pctwater.com/. It is important to keep in mind, however, that this report isn't guaranteed to be accurate every time. In past years, trail angels have maintained water caches, but you should *never* rely on someone else for your water, especially because you don't feel like carrying a few extra pounds.

Suggestion: To adjust to the lack of water, my advice is to err on the side of caution - carry more than you think you'll need, as the alternative is downright dangerous, or at best, more stressful. Over time, you'll hone in on how much water you require under specific temperatures and over specific distances.

The point here is not to outline every instance where you should expect to battle thirst, but more so to demonstrate that the lack of water is going to be a major obstacle, especially early on.

The Weather

The weather affects far more than your personal appearance[78] and gear setup; it can also force you to adjust your mileage to the current conditions. For example, let's say you plan on hiking 23 miles one day in order to make it to the next town for lunch the following day, but it turned out to be exceptionally hot that day. You decide to take a three-hour siesta, so that 23 mile day turned into a 15 mile

---

which are not always reliable. Here's a bit more data fun: there are 18 total stretches of 20 miles or more without water on the PCT, 8 stretches of 25 miles, 3 stretches of 40 miles (again using the same caveat as above). Thanks to Guthook for sharing this data!

[78] If you're going to go the short sleeve and/or shorts route, expect some world class tan lines.

day. Or heavy rain came through the night before and washed out part of the trail and took down most of the trees with it. Maybe there was a snowstorm in the Sierra. Or there's a fire near the trail in Oregon, and while the trail is still open, the air is filled with smoke, straining your eyes and making breathing difficult[79]. Navigating in those conditions takes far longer than you expect, which will result in a decrease in mileage.

Suggestion: Weather will very likely require you to adjust your hiking plans several times over the course of your thru-hike. In the desert, it's common for hikers to take a break during the hottest parts of the day and then continue hiking late into the night when it's much cooler. Waiting out the sun and heat might not be for you, in which case you might explore the option of hiking with an umbrella, or just ensuring ample sun protection for your face and neck. In the case of heavy snow or rain, you might consider waiting out a storm to pass before entering that section of trail. Too much smoke from forest fires might cause you to hike particular sections in a different order (or direction) than you had originally planned.

Shipping Food

There are definitely places to resupply along the trail, but it's also very common to mail food ahead to yourself. In some places, I would say it's absolutely necessary. To get a better idea of where to send mail drops, check out the 2015 thru-hiker's survey from halfwayanywhere.com referenced several times throughout this book[80]. Adapting your hiking schedule to a post office can be tricky. Knowing the hours of the post offices you're sending packages to is highly encouraged, but even with this knowledge, there may come a time when you miss this window. Arriving after operating hours is frustrating and can be a major source of stress if you're trying to hike a fixed number of miles that day or the following. If there are no other resupply options nearby,

---

[79] Not just a hypothetical. This happened to me.

[80] Or just go here http://bit.ly/PCT-Survey (case sensitive)

you'll be forced to wait until the post office opens, requiring a shift in plans.

Suggestion: You can send mail drops to businesses with more flexible hours. There are many locations along the PCT other than post offices where you can send packages. These include convenience or camp stores, trail angels' houses, and motels. Some of these locations have pick-up fees, typically only the remote camp stores; these charges are usually nominal (an exception is Vermillion Valley Resort which charges $22).

You could try sending fewer mail drops and resupplying at grocery stores and convenience stores more often on the trail; each has its own relative pros and cons. If you decide during your hike that you prefer mail drops, you can easily send food ahead to future stops from the trail.

When I hiked the PCT, I found it helpful to have a spreadsheet of each of my resupply points, which included the hours of operations, phone number and any fees charged. I carried it with me the entire hike and had several occasions where I called ahead to confirm when the store was closing (sometimes there are discrepancies among sources for the open and closing times), or to let them know I was way behind on my ETA (a.k.a. don't feed my food to the marmots!).

Gear

Depending on the weather each hiking season, the gear can fluctuate. Perhaps you'll add a couple warmer layers for Washington or you'll forego the ice axe and micro spikes in the Sierra due to a low snow year. You might decide you need some serious insect repellent and/or mosquito-proof clothing[81], cap, and head net for when the mosquitoes strike, which can be anywhere in the Sierra and beyond.

Gear changes will also depend on personal preference. Maybe the tarp isn't quite working out as you expected,

---

[81] Exofficio's BugsAway apparel line is a good example. This should be in addition to a bug net during the thick of mosquito season.

making the idea of a tent more appealing. Or, perhaps you prefer using water bottles instead of a bladder.

Suggestion: Likely obvious, but you're not going to need all of your gear throughout your entire hike. Your snow gear won't serve you until you reach Kennedy Meadows South, around mile 700. That's not to say you won't see any snow in the high desert (2015 did), but chances are you won't need the ice axe until the Sierra. Consider whether you really want to be *that* person in the 100-degree heat with an ice axe.

Many hikers hang onto their cold weather clothing (thermals, puffy jacket, warm hat) for the remainder of their hike, some send these warmer layers ahead to Oregon. At that point in your hike you'll have more than enough knowledge of the gear that works for you and what you'll need for the trail ahead. Most pick up more gear in Washington, as it's likely you'll experience cooler, wetter conditions.

A quick note about bugs - the mosquitoes can be really bad in the Sierra and Oregon. It all depends on the year, but I would suggest being prepared with plenty of repellent and/or suitable bug clothing. Some prefer using DEET, others opt for a chemical free approach and wear more mosquito-proof clothing, which is to say, woven fabric instead of knit. I hiked the entire trail with a bug net (it weighs almost nothing). Some people spray their clothes with permethrin prior to leaving for the trail. Since permethrin lasts for a limited time (6 washings or 42 days of sun exposure), you'll get the best bang for your buck by sending your treated clothes to Kennedy Meadows South[82].

Snorkel does a fantastic job outlining your gear needs in the next chapter, so for the sake of avoiding redundancy, I'll simply encourage you to read and reread that chapter when considering your gear.

The Terrain

---

[82] Buying clothes pre-treated with permethrin at the factory-level tends to last longer.

When I think back to my time on the PCT, I sometimes feel I was on several different trails because each environment felt so different compared to the prior sections. I believe the hike can be broken up into five sections of terrain: the desert, Sierra Nevada, Northern California, Oregon, and Washington.

The desert offers smooth trail over gradual hills and a lot of exposure to the sun. If you're new to backpacking, you might find hiking here somewhat challenging. If you were already active before the trail, it's likely your biggest struggle will come from the heat and sun exposure. Although the grade is forgiving, hot weather will intensify the difficulty. I stopped often to shake rocks and sand out from my shoes. For this reason, you may want to consider investing in gaiters as Liz suggests in the next chapter.

Then there's the Sierra Nevada, which is almost the complete opposite of the desert. This section is incredibly raw, rugged, and steep. Northbound thru-hikers gain elevation pretty quickly after leaving Kennedy Meadows South and enter the Sierra Nevada. You'll face rigorous climbs combined with rocky terrain at a much higher elevation. Your previous backpacking experience will affect your perception of just how *steep*, *rocky*, or *challenging* you find the terrain, but compared to the desert, you will feel like you are in a new world.

Shortly after exiting the Sierra, I recall literally seeing the sharp peaks giving way to a more moderate grade. There are still some decent climbs, but it's generally milder than what you have just hiked through. This continues through Northern California. This portion has a lot of vegetation and is very green.

Oregon presents some of the PCT's easiest hiking from a terrain standpoint. While most of the three previous sections of the trail are exposed, Oregon has many extended stretches under tree cover. The adjustment here is largely psychological; getting used to not having expansive views or seeing as much direct sunlight can be a shock to your system.

For me, hiking through Washington brought back flashbacks of the Sierra: sharp climbs, big mountains in the distance, a kind of unrefined quality to the landscape. You spend a lot of time around 6,000 feet, unlike the Sierra where you're above 10,000 feet almost every day. While the actual elevation doesn't compare to the Sierra, the burn my legs felt walking up those mountains was all too familiar. In Washington you're still climbing thousands of feet over the course of a day, you just have more oxygen to do it.

Suggestion: Your mileage will be cut considerably once you cross from the desert into the Sierra and again from Oregon into Washington. The key is acceptance. What was easy terrain for you at one point in time might prove to be a struggle later on down the trail. There may be points several weeks into your hike where you think, "This is easy! I've mastered this hiking thing!" Two hundred miles later you might be wondering if you're going to make it up the next mountain.

What's easy on the legs may not be easy on the brain- the same formula follows for the challenging stretches. In fact, many hikers will tell you the most difficult sections were also their favorite. My best advice is to embrace the diversity of the trail. Some sections may not be your favorite at the time, but you will come to embrace these stretches more as time passes. This has certainly been the case for me. Embrace the possibility that the most challenging section for you might not be a steep, rocky section of trail, but instead the seemingly casual stroll through the woods.

Your Mentality

Each of the aforementioned elements converges at a single point: modifying your mentality. Like anything in life, unexpected events are going to occur and you'll have to adjust to those situations while you're on the trail. We mentioned some of these possibilities in previous chapters, but it's impossible and unnecessary to cover *every* scenario that could effect a thru-hiker's journey. The trail doesn't protect you from day-to-day life. It can be easy to fall into a negative space when things aren't going your way- when the weather isn't ideal, when your feet are screaming at you, when you have an argument with a loved one on the phone, when the 4,000 feet of elevation gain over what should have been an "easy" day takes every ounce of your energy and then some, but at the end of the day, your outlook is the one constant you can control..

Suggestion: I've always found my mentality to be both my biggest liability and my greatest asset. As a friend said to me, "Discovering your own adaptability and strengthening it is the biggest reward of the trail." I agree. Being able to alter the way you view the situation at hand is the light through the trees. There are many unknowns when it comes to hiking the PCT - *having stretches where you have to adapt is not one of them.* You will absolutely have times during your hike where it's vital to adjust and it's in your best interest to be aware of and ready for those moments.

Expect the unexpected. Recognize that although there is a lot out of your control, you are in the driver's seat for the one thing that matters most, your outlook. You have the toolset for becoming an emotional ninja at this point, but this is just a final, friendly reminder, *shit happens.*

In Summary

Ultimately, the demands for adaptability are mere details in the broader scope of your upcoming thru-hike. You can spend hours developing a thorough gear setup for each individual section only to discover that you'll learn a different method that better suits your needs once out on the trail. This chapter isn't designed to offer you one absolute method for how to adjust on the trail, although I've included some tips to get you off on the right foot.

Instead, this chapter's goal is to alert you that there will be times when you need to pivot psychologically. Whether this is caused by water accessibility, gear needs, weather, and/or resupply strategy, the PCT is going to test you. The crux of your ability to pass or fail still resides in strength of the gear between your ears, which, by reading this book, will be top of the line.

Chapter 12 – Liz "Snorkel" Thomas' Gear Chapter

This is not a gear book. However, in the process of interacting with thousands of thru-hikers, I've come to learn that gear is consistently a top concern, and rightfully so. Although the most important aspect of successfully completing a thru-hike is the gear between your ears, the gear in your pack (and on your body) will also play a significant role. To neglect this topic would be doing you a disservice, and we are here to serve. To be of *best* service, we have sought the wisdom of one of the most accomplished and knowledgeable thru-hikers out there.

Enter Liz "Snorkel" Thomas.

I first met Snorkel on the Appalachian Trail in 2011 at the Holiday Inn in Daleville, Virginia, which is roughly one third of the way through the trail. At the time, the group I was hiking with was moving at solid clip. The three of us had all started our hikes on the same date, March 21. It was uncommon to meet other thru-hikers who started after us, and in those rare instances, it was by a few days at most. As dictated by the *unspoken thru-hiker's guide to small talk*—exchanging trail names and discussing the forecast—I asked Snorkel when she began her thru-hike. "April 15th," she said. This was nearly *four weeks* after we had started! What came out of her mouth had to have been a mistake, I thought. I repeated the date back to her, punctuated with a question mark. "Yup," she responded casually.

At first I assumed there were only two explanations for what I had just heard—either this person is prone to embellishing, or she is downright crazy. Hiking more than seven hundred miles in roughly half the time it took us seemed unfathomable. A third explanation quickly became apparent when I saw Liz pick up her backpack—*she was telling the truth.* Her fully loaded pack looked like a daypack. At a point in the trail where most hikers' gaits resemble that of a tender-footed zombie[83], Snorkel whipped her fifteen-pound pack over her shoulders, said, "Well, good luck with your hike", and, with springs in her legs, spryly marched through the automatic hotel doors on her way to setting the women's self-supported A.T. speed record[84] of 80 days and 13.5 hours[85].

This is only the tip of the iceberg in terms of Snorkel's backpacking resume. She's completed the Triple Crown (the Pacific Crest, Appalachian, and Continental Divide Trails), has been featured countless times in Backpacker Magazine, serves as Vice President of the American Long Distance Hiking Association–West, and has earned a master's from Yale and a fellowship from the Doris Duke Charitable Trust for her research on long distance hiking trails, conservation, and gateway communities.

In other words, Liz is a certified backpacking badass.

This is why I'm thrilled she's taken the reins to offer you an *extremely* thorough outline on how to pack for your PCT thru-hike. When you're done reading this book, be sure to check out Liz's blog (eathomas.com) to glean even more backpacking wisdom. And when you're done with this chapter, head to the appendices for her full gear checklist to assist in your gear acquisition process.

Without further ado, I gladly present to you:

---

[83] Lovingly referred to as the "hiker hobble" on the trail.

[84] This was broken in 2015 by Heather "Anish" Anderson.

[85] For reference, the average thru-hike on the AT is somewhere between five and six months.

Liz "Snorkel" Thomas' PCT Gear Chapter

On the PCT, the odds are against you succeeding. As mentioned previously in this book, best estimates say that between 50-60% of aspiring thru-hikers fall short of their goal of completing the entire trail. There are a lot of aspects that contribute to whether you will succeed or fail. You have little control over most of these—weather, water conditions, and wildfires being some of the most obvious. For these variables, you only have control in how you react. But gear is the one aspect of your thru-hike that you have *total* control over.

Sure, hikers have finished the PCT carrying old school, heavy, traditional gear. And just because a hiker has state-of-the-art gear doesn't mean s/he is a slam dunk for finishing.

But choosing the right gear is a (relatively) easy way to stack those odds in your favor. That's why this chapter is set up to give you a leg up on the trail learning curve, potentially sparing you from unnecessary pain and injury and saving you boatloads of money.

Why You Should Trust Me

With over 16 different end-to-end thru-hikes and more than 15,000 miles of long distance hiking, I've had *a lot* of time to think about gear. I was honored with the Triple Crown of Hiking by the American Long Distance Hiking Association–West for completing the AT, PCT, and CDT with continuous footsteps (keep that in mind if you're ever considering yellow-blazing—no shortcuts allowed here). From 2011-2015, I held the women's unassisted speed record on the AT. I've tried lots of gear models in different terrains, climates, and weather, and on established trails as well as on not-at-all-established routes—including two routes I pioneered (the Chinook Trail and Wasatch Range Traverse, which I did solo). As far as the PCT goes, I thru-hiked it in 2009 and will have put together another end-to-end hike by the end of 2016. I also wrote my master's thesis on the PCT, so I've spent a lot—and I mean A LOT—of time getting familiar with that trail.

My gear philosophy

I may know the PCT. I may know long distance hiking. But no matter how much any purported "expert" may know, you know *you* better than anyone else. The gear tips below won't belabor you about what works best for me or other PCT hikers. This chapter also isn't about letting you off the hook on gear decision-making. I wrote this so you have the criteria to judge for *yourself* what kind of gear will work for *you*.

How to Buy Gear

If you're more than a year out from your thru-hike, *resist the temptation to purchase gear now.* Technology changes. Models change. Prices drop. I've been suckered into a smokin' deal more than once myself (in fact, my first thru-hike included nothing but REI Garage Sale gear—a poor choice, if you're wondering). Often when I buy a piece of clearance gear, six months later, it's moldering in the garage, maybe having only been used once. That's $300 that could have been turned into trail ice cream instead!

Yes, gear can be expensive. You can expect to spend between $2,000 and $3,000 on gear before your feet touch the trail. But think of your gear as your rent: your pack and its contents are your home for 4-6 months. A Dyneema Composite Fiber (aka cuben fiber) shelter could set you back $600. That sounds like a lot to spend until you realize that's $4 a night. You'll have a hard time finding a hostel at that price anywhere!

Of course, you can put together a gear kit for a lot less than the sticker price at your local outfitter. Used gear can be easily tracked down on the Internet, and lots of discounted-but-still-awesome items (including a few you can make out of trash) can be found during holiday sales. In this chapter, I'll give advice on gear items you can get on the cheap without sacrificing too much quality.

The biggest obstacle to your gear-buying task is trying to only purchase one of each major item. Yes, you would think you'd only need one backpack to hike the PCT, yet far too many thru-hikers find themselves disliking the gear they start with and upgrading during their hike. This is usually because they realize after a couple hundred miles in the gear they have just doesn't work for them. On my first AT hike, I bought a new backpack, new poles, and more pairs of shoes than I could possibly wear over the miles I was covering. When all was said and done, the sticker price of that hike was at least $2,000 more than I had expected. *If you get your gear right the first time, you save money.*

Do your research, practice with gear at home and on shorter trips, and make sure that when you hit the trail, you know and love every piece of gear that's on your back.

Why Go Light on the PCT?

As this book has made clear, the PCT is a long trail with some major ups and downs. You'll be hitting some of the most extreme ecosystems in the Lower 48.

Having ultralight (or at least light) gear makes it easier for you to be nimble, quick, and safe when the weather turns nasty, especially when you're above treeline at places like Bighorn Flats. With a light pack, you'll be able to focus more on the scenery, your friends, navigation, and safety instead of putting all your mental and physical energy towards moving your pack. Carrying a lighter pack also puts you in a better position to help others if you need to carry an injured friend's gear or rush to get emergency help. In contrast, carrying a heavy pack is inefficient—it requires you eat more food to power your body, which in turn requires you to carry more food, which means you'll have an even heavier pack.

Yes, people have done the PCT with heavy packs. I'm friends with a bunch of guys and gals who thru-hiked in the 1970s who hefted the equivalent of a small human on their backs. But all of them say that if they were to hike the trail again today, there is no way they'd keep carrying their 80 pound packs. Back then, they carried those packs out of necessity: the technology wasn't anywhere near what it is now. Today you can easily hike the PCT with a 15 pound base weight[86]. Technology improves for a reason, and that reason is to make our lives easier.

Two thousand six hundred fifty miles, multiplied by 450,000 feet of elevation gain, equals a *lot* of pressure in your knees, ankles, and feet. Joints, especially in the feet and ankles, will rub and fracture at a faster rate when you have a heavier pack (especially if you also hike more miles or hike at a faster speed than your body can handle). These are the types of injuries that not only take people off trail for good, but could also ride with you long after the hike is over, even for the rest of your life.

So How Do I Go Lighter?

Just like losing weight off your belly, losing weight from your pack requires monitoring and putting your gear on a scale. Before you buy, set up a list of your "dream gear". Create a spreadsheet (see our gear checklist in this book) and list each item, its weight, and its cost. Adding in a simple Sum Formula[87], you should be able to figure out what each individual category of gear weighs and, more importantly, what your total base weight will be. Now, take a long hard look at those numbers and think: "Can I reasonably scale back on this weight and stay within my price range?" When you have crunched the numbers, look to remove any redundant items, and consider which items have multiple uses. Great examples of multi-use gear are hiking poles used as tent poles, gloves used as potholders, and a bandana used to pre-filter water, just to name a few.

As I mentioned earlier, the more you know about hiking gear, the lighter your pack can be. If you're able to get in some short overnight trips or day trips, invite some hiker friends who carry a lighter pack than you do; ask them about their gear and have them teach you to use lighter

---

[86] A term that refers to all hiking gear minus food, water, and what you're normally wearing.

[87] for those who don't speak fluent nerd, this is a Microsoft Excel formula which automatically adds totals. If you don't know how to do this, a calculator will do

items safely. These experienced ultralight hikers can also guide you to the gear you *really* need and which gear is a semi-pointless upsell from a profit-seeking salesperson at the outfitter.

The Big Four

If you're just starting to collect backpacking gear for your hike or are thinking about upgrading some older items, the number one way to reduce pack weight is to get your Big Four items as light as possible.

The four major categories of backpacking gear (aka the Big Four) are your sleeping bag, sleeping pad, shelter, and backpack. These items often take up 65%-80% of the weight of a backpacker's gear. I aim to have each of these items weigh less than two pounds apiece. That makes for some easy math: if each of my Big Four items weighs in at two pounds, the heaviest four items in my pack will weigh eight pounds total.

Carrying the Right Gear for the Conditions

For an April-to-September thru-hike of the PCT, you'll likely hit temperatures as low as the teens on a few occasions and as high as 110°F or higher. You'll be walking through desert, snow, temperate rain forest, and everything in between. Most hikers find the PCT to be a drier trail—at least when compared to the Appalachian Trail—but when it does rain, it's often a cold, biting rain that makes rain gear essential for avoiding hypothermia[88]. The dry western climate can also be confusing for many hikers—expect some high temperatures on sunny days and a major temperature drop at night when the sun dips below the horizon (40°F changes aren't uncommon).

So how do you plan for such extreme conditions? Thru-hikers have a few options. You may consider having two sets of key gear items—one for the colder conditions and one for warmer conditions. Mail yourself the cold weather

---

[88] There's a famous old song with the lyrics, "It never rains in California/but it pours man, it pours."

gear when you get to the Sierra and either ship your warm weather gear home or to a pick-up location in Northern California. When you arrive in Oregon, you may need to do this trade again. Whether you're bouncing your heavy-duty parka to the cold spots or your 40°F sleeping bag to the hot spots on the trail, the post office can help ensure that you have comfortable gear over the course of your hike.

If you're on a budget and need one piece of gear to do it all, choose items that are versatile. These items are not going to be perfect in all conditions, but with a little tweaking, they will get the job done no matter what gets thrown your way.

Sleeping Bag

Sleep is hugely important to thru-hikers—it's the time when your body recovers and rebuilds muscles from the daily onslaught of physical activity. If your body is too busy trying to keep itself warm and comfortable, it's going to have fewer resources to repair itself.

That's why, if you absolutely must skimp on one piece of gear, your sleeping bag should be the *last* option. Remember, you're going to spend at least 8 hours a day in your bag for months on end—you might as well spend the extra money to ensure you're getting something you love. Also, a good sleeping bag will last ten years or more, making it an investment that will last for years after you have stepped off the PCT.

If you can only afford one bag, many hikers (myself included) found a 20°F down bag to do the trick in all seasons. During hot nights in Northern California, I slept on top of the bag and inside of a bug bivy. When it snowed six inches in the Sierra, I was warm in my bag as long as I was also wearing all my dry clothes (including my down jacket). Surprisingly, the desert nights were cold enough that I was happy with a 20°F bag, but I also tend to sleep "cold."

That last fact is actually overlooked fairly often: when choosing a bag, think about whether you tend to sleep warm or cold at home. Women and older men tend to sleep colder, so choose your bag accordingly. Some people who sleep hot or don't roll around a lot at night prefer a quilt sleeping system, which is essentially like the top half of a sleeping bag. By carrying a quilt, you could save some significant weight and money, but make sure you like the design first: switching to a quilt requires some getting used to and may not be suited for those on their first backpacking adventure.

Sleeping bags work by puffing out and creating a wall of insulation between you and the cold air. Your body heat warms up the air inside the bag, which creates a warm chamber. If you have a lot of empty space in your sleeping bag, it will take longer to warm up all the air inside. Thus, you'll feel warmer more quickly in a bag that is as snug as you can get without feeling claustrophobic. You'll also want a bag that's large enough to keep parts of your body (especially your feet) from hitting the sides or end of the bag— this could compress the down, which reduces its insulating features). Pricier bags will often have features sewn into the inside the bag that keep the down insulation in one place and, as a result, keep you warmer.

The majority of PCT thru-hikers go with down sleeping bags, and so should you if you have the cash and know-how to keep your bag dry. When compared to synthetic insulation, down has a much better warmth-to-weight ratio, lasts longer, and is more compressible. The PCT is a drier trail, so the chances of your bag getting wet are far less than on the AT. However, don't let your sleeping bag get wet, even if you splurged on the pricey "waterproof treated" down—down will lose its insulating abilities when wet or moist, which means you'll be wet, cold, and miserable for an entire night (or potentially longer if rain is in the forecast). Protect your bag from rain, snow, and condensation by checking out the "Gear Care" section of this chapter.

Examples of awesome bags[89]**:** Western Mountaineering 20 Degree Ultralight (what I carried on the Triple Crown), Montbell Downhugger #2 (suitable for warm sleepers),

---

[89] We've included a list of all of the recommended products and will continue to update this list for you at http://bit.ly/pctgear

Katabatic Alsek 22, Marmot Plasma 15, Feathered Friends Hummingbird UL 20, Enlightened Equipment Revelation 20 degree quilt, and Zpacks 20 degree quilt.

Sleeping Pad

Staying warm at night is a two-part equation based on how warm your bag is and how much insulation you have under you. Sleeping pads aren't just there to be a buffer between you and the rocky ground—they insulate you from the cold soil (and snow) beneath you.

You don't need a super thick pad to thru-hike the PCT during the summer. Check the manufacturers' specs for the R-value (a term used to measure insulating capabilities of a sleeping pad's materials). Reading an R-value is simple: the higher the number, the warmer the pad. Most regular season thru-hikers find themselves to be relatively comfortable using sleeping pads with an R-factor between 2.2 to 3.2.

Inflatable pads tend to be warmer and more comfortable, but keep in mind that the PCT is located in a cactus-filled desert: if you decide to go inflatable, be prepared to baby your pad to prevent it from popping. Using a ground sheet, packing a bathtub floor tent, bivy, or a combination of these elements is a good method for protecting your pad. However, no matter how careful you are, carry a repair kit—Mother Nature loves to toy with the emotions of headstrong hikers.

Foam sleeping pads will be more durable than inflatable ones and are well suited to those who enjoy cowboy camping. These pads will slowly compress over time, making them less warm and comfortable over the course of your hike, but they are cheap—you could easily have a few on standby that you send for when your current one wears out. Closed cell foam pads are lighter in weight and can also work well as makeshift frames in frameless backpacks (more on that later). During my first thru of the PCT, I carried the foam Gossamer Gear Nightlite torso pad. For my second hike, I switched to an inflatable pad.

Examples of Awesome Inflatable Sleeping Pads: Neo Air XLite, Sea to Summit UltraLight Mat, Klymit Inertia X Frame, Exped Synmat Hyperlite

Examples of Awesome Foam Sleeping Pads: Cascade Designs Z-Lite, Cascade Designs Z-Lite Sol, Gossamer Gear Nightlight, $5 Blue Foamy You See At Discount Camping Stores (multiple brands)

Shelters

Let's get one thing perfectly clear: do not attempt to hike any part the PCT—even southern California—without a shelter. You could wake up to deep snow in southern California, and if you think you've experienced heavy rain, just wait until you've gotten to Washington. The PCT often rolls high above treeline, so a shelter can be just as useful for wind protection as it is for precipitation. Trust me: shelters are essential equipment for a PCT thru-hike.

So when considering shelters, your first goal should be to find something that is easy for you to set up. After selecting a few options, watch some YouTube videos on how each shelter is set up to gauge if it seems doable for you. An even better option is to find some experienced thru-hikers in your area, go on an overnighter with them, and have them teach you how to set up their shelter.

Next, consider what sort of coverage and protection you want. Fully-enclosed shelters tend to offer more protection, but can result in significant amounts of condensation inside your tent. This happens when water droplets from your breath or from the air form on the *inside* of the tent. Many hikers unfamiliar with condensation have woken up to water dripping from their shelter ceiling and thought that their shelter was leaking.

A tarp shelter is a great choice for minimizing condensation, as it is designed with ventilation in mind. If you have a lot of experience picking out protected campsites and setting up a tarp in various configurations, you don't need as much coverage and will experience less condensation as a result. Plenty of hybrid models exist as well, combining the ventilation of a tarp with some of the structure and stability of a traditional tent.

If you currently lack the skill set required to set up a tarp or hybrid tent in a variety of weather conditions and don't have time to learn before hitting the trail, it may be worth considering a freestanding tent. Freestanding tents use dedicated tent poles to remain upright and don't typically require guylines for support. These tents typically come in two varieties: single wall, which only have a single layer of fabric separating you from the elements; and double wall, which often have a thinner inner wall (sometimes just a bug screen) and a thicker outer wall to protect from wind and precipitation. Single wall tents will be lighter, but double walled tents can often be more straightforward to set up. Some double walled tents will also be better at keeping condensation out of the inside of your tent, as air will be able to move between the two walls and carry away moisture. Ultimately, your campsite selection will play just as an important role in how much condensation you get, regardless of whether you carry a single walled or double walled shelter.

Speaking of keeping things out of your tent, many hikers find that Tuolumne Meadows up to Oregon can rival the tropics for mosquitoes. Whether the bug netting is built into your shelter, is removable and comes separately, or is part of a system with your bivy or a bug headnet, you will need a bug plan for at least part of this trip.

Another aspect to consider: many tents, tarps, and hybrid tents are meant to be used with trekking poles as part of the shelter's support system. These kind of shelters reduce the overall weight of gear you will carry. While setup can sometimes be a bit more tricky, the weight savings might be worth it for you in the end.

An excellent shelter has a taut setup that doesn't have loose, flapping material that will flail in the wind during the night. Water will also roll right off these shelters during storms. You can tell pretty quickly which shelters will easily resist wind and water just from looking at photos on gear websites. Even so, some designs are better (read: tauter) than others, so inspect your final shelter choices in person if at all possible. When you have made your choice, be sure to practice setting up your shelter in a variety of terrains and weather conditions and make sure you know how to make your ridgelines very tight. Otherwise, your shelter will flap in the wind like a flag, which isn't great when you're trying to score some hard-earned shuteye.

Most PCT hikers carry a sheet of Polycro or Tyvek to use as a groundsheet underneath their tent. This will either protect your shelter's bathtub floor from the harsh ground of the PCT, or will be the floor of your floorless shelter. This groundsheet can also be used to set your sleeping pad on when you're cowboy camping. After a rain, you can set the groundsheet on the wet ground and dry your gear on top of it. Some PCT hikers write "Hiker to Town" on the back of their groundsheet to aid in hitchhiking. A durable groundsheet is truly a PCT hiker's multi-talented friend.

Whatever shelter you choose, make sure it is big enough for you *and* all your gear. Many solo hikers like rolling with a 2-person shelter just to have a little more sprawling room, especially if they have wet gear that they'd rather not have against their sleeping bag all night. Be sure to look at the height of the shelter as well: many shelters don't have room to sit fully upright, especially if you are over six feet tall. However, keep in mind that a bigger shelter will require more ground space, making it difficult to set up in small campsites.

Perhaps even more so than the other items in the Big Four, shelters are a prime example of how knowledge and skill can save you some money and weight. Shelters that look more tent-like will cost more, whereas shelters that look more tarp-like tend to cost less. If you're super talented at setting up tarps and choosing protected campsites, you can save a lot of money (and weight) by using a simple flat tarp (just be sure to get silnylon or even cuben, not the blue tarpaulins you can find at Walmart).

Examples of Awesome Shelters: Z-Packs Solo-Plus shelter, Tarptent Rainbow, Mountain Laurel Designs Solomid, Six Moons Designs Skyscrape Trekker and Six Moons Lunar Solo

Double-walled shelters seen on trail: Big Agnes Cooper Spur UL 2, Big Agnes Fly Creek UL 2, MSR Hubba NX

Backpack

Features to Look for in a Thru-Hiking Backpack

Capacity: A backpack should be the last piece of gear you purchase, and it should be one of two pieces of gear (after your sleeping bag) that you don't skimp the dollars on. By waiting to purchase this last, you'll ensure that all your gear, food, and water will fit comfortably inside. Remember, you'll essentially be living in your pack for months, so think of it as your trusty companion and temporary life partner. Just like a spouse, do not settle for "just ok."

Before you buy a pack, get a reasonable idea of what your overall pack weight will be (include all your gear, food and water). Most pack companies clearly state the weight limits for each model; if you carry more than this listed weight limit, your pack will be uncomfortable and could potentially become damaged.

Your pack weight, loading limits, and personal strength/comfort/tolerance will help you determine whether you get a frameless, internal frame, or external frame backpack. Frameless packs use your sleeping pad as the "frame" of your pack. They work well for those with the lightest loads (typically 20 pounds or less). Some "semi-internal frame" packs include metal stays that can help distribute a modest load (typically 30 pounds or less).

Internal frame packs have the frame sewn into the pack itself and can carry significantly more weight (typically 30 pounds or more). These are some of the most common types of packs you will experience on the trail, as they provide substantial support while still remaining relatively lightweight.

External frame packs are rare on the PCT these days (except for hipsters opting for retro-gear). These packs are designed to carry the heaviest loads and distribute the weight somewhat evenly. The side effect of offering such substantial support is, unfortunately, a substantial pack weight.

Most PCT hikers carry a backpack that holds between 40 and 65 liters (with the main pouch containing 30-50 liters of space—the remaining capacity is held by secondary pockets, lids, mesh pockets, etc.). For the majority of the trail, this amount of space is more than adequate for the gear and supplies you will be carrying. In the Sierra, however, most hikers are carrying *at* their space limit, so the weight of their pack is typically over the loading suggestions for comfort. Most hikers decide to just deal with it for the (relatively) short amount of time they will be spending in the Sierra. If you have the money and are worried about comfort, you can always send yourself a bigger pack to carry just for this section.

Because rules and regulations for the Sierra require that you carry a bear canister, make sure your pack can fit your bear canister inside or, if not, can easily and securely attach to the outside of your pack (call pack manufacturer and ask them just to be sure).

Lastly, if you're going to carry an ice axe for the Sierra, make sure your pack has an ice axe loop.

Fit and Comfort: With a backpack, you want to find something that fits well when your gear is fully loaded (note; that it should be all of your *actual* gear, food and water—simulating this with dumbbells or some other stand-in doesn't convey the density or feel of a loaded pack in the same way). Any small annoyance you feel when you try it on at the store could potentially turn into painful chafing 700 sweaty miles up the trail.

The problem with getting the fit right on your pack is that most ultralight gear companies are "cottage industries," which means they are not available in brick and mortar gear stores. To make up for it, they do have generous return policies and detailed instructions on where on your body to measure to find the pack that fits you. Many of these companies also show up at trail events (PCT Kick Off, PCT Days, the American Long Distance Hiking Association—West Gathering, etc.) so that hikers can have an opportunity to feel, see, and touch their items.

When inspecting potential packs, look for comfy shoulder straps that don't slip off the ends of your shoulders. Some gear companies offer different shoulder strap designs suited for women and men under 5'10". Many hikers—especially women—enjoy having a padded hip belt to help distribute the weight.

Your pack's comfort level is determined by the pack's design, the weight of your pack, and how well you distribute the weight of your pack. Do some research on how best to pack your gear (which items go in first, what should go in last) to maximize the comfort of what is on your back. Again, YouTube can be a useful source for packing tips and examples.

Accessibility: Most PCT hikers like to be able to reach their water bottles, lip balm, snacks, etc., without having to take their pack off. Put the pack on and see how easy it is to reach around for your water bottle and other pockets. If you can't reach it at home, chances are that it will become insanely annoying when you're thirsty on trail and too lazy to take off your pack. Little annoyances can frequently become amplified when you're out in the woods alone and that's all that you're thinking about for hours (sometimes days) at a time, so give your mind a break and avoid the things that are already irritating off the trail.

Durability: A backpack should reasonably last you the length of the PCT—if not longer—with good care (again, see the care section). Most gear companies will repair or replace your pack for free if you do not get a full thru-hike out of it. Overloading is the most common reason for pack failure— be sure to find something that truly will hold all the weight of your gear, food, and water on a typical day.

Sweat, ultraviolet light (read: sunshine), spiky rocks, and cactus—all things your pack will encounter on the PCT—will also create points of weakness in your pack's fabric. The salt from your sweat and UV rays from the sun will slowly abrade the pack's material, so start keeping an eye for thinning or frayed fabrics. And of course, take care not to set your pack on rough rocks or cactus.

Breathability: Some internal frame pack designs feature ventilation in the back panel (the part against your back) of the pack, which helps keep your back cool. If you're going with a frameless pack, you will have the pack panel right against your back; thus, consider the breathability of the pack's fabric. Expect limited breathability from the untreated fabrics that are also used to make tarps, such as cuben fiber (aka CTF3, Dyneema Composite Fabric, Dyneema Non-woven, or possibly another name by this point), a popular, expensive fabric used in ultralight gear.

Weight: In the end, most PCT thru-hikers in the last few years carry packs that weigh between one and three pounds. The more extras they have, the heavier they will be.

Examples of great ultralight packs (frameless or very moderately framed): Gossamer Gear Kumo, Mountain Laurel Designs PROPHET, ULA Circuit, Z-Packs Arc Blast

Examples of slightly heavier-duty packs popular for thru-hikers: Gossamer Gear Mariposa, Osprey Exos 48, Granite Gear Virga 2 or Crown 60, Six Moon Designs Fusion

Stoves

Now that we have put the Big Four behind us, we can get to gear options that might have a multitude of styles and/or options or might be entirely optional. Perhaps the clearest example of this is what has been left out of many peoples backcountry kitchen: a backpacking stove.

I went stoveless on my 2009 thru-hike of the PCT. My rationale was that the desert is often warm and a hot meal is not missed as much. Hot food requires water to boil, and I didn't always have water to spare. The PCT is also especially prone to wildfire, so going stoveless was another way to make sure I wasn't the one that invoked Smokey the Bear's wrath.

For my second time on the PCT, however, I carried a stove. I love having the comfort of hot meals and drinks at night. On my thru of the PCT, I hated eating cold food while I watched my friends eat hot meals. In the Sierra, I was freezing after walking in the snow all day long, and eating re-soaked dehydrated refried beans was such a letdown.

So when considering whether or not to carry a stove, know this: having hiked the PCT both ways, and I definitely preferred having a stove with me.

The kind of stove you carry will depend on fire regulations, fuel availability (some fuels are easier to find in trail towns than others), and personal preference.

During high fire years on the PCT, Forest Service regulations may require hikers to carry stoves with on/off valves. For most thru-hikers, this means canister stoves (white gas stoves tend to be way too heavy for weight-conscious thru-hikers). Canister stoves tend to be heavier than other options but they also cook faster. If you carry a canister stove, make sure to use your guidebooks to help plan out a fuel resupply option. Check to make sure that canisters are sold in the town(s) in which you'll be resupplying. If not, you may be able to mail yourself a fuel canister, but plan ahead—it will have to be declared to the shipping service and sent via ground shipping.

Historically, during wet years, many PCT hikers enjoy using alcohol stoves. These can often be made for free out of garbage like cat food or soda cans. You can use the available-at-every-gas-station HEET as fuel (this is gas line anti-freeze—always use the yellow bottle, not the red).

If you decide to use an alcohol stove, always put your hand near the stove to feel for heat before adding more alcohol or touching the stove. Be careful not to accidentally kick your stove over. PCT hikers and their alcohol stoves have caused multiple forest fires on the PCT—not to mention ruining thousands of dollars of their gear and giving themselves or other hikers massively painful get-off-the-trail-RIGHT-NOW skin burns. For this reason, even though thru-hikers can be mavericks, it's important to watch the YouTube videos and read instructions on how to use an alcohol stove before you hit the trail. A prepared hiker is a third-degree-burn free hiker.

Whatever stove you go with, the PCT is a windy trail, so be sure to get a good windscreen. I like the Trail Designs Caldera Cone, which is a dual purpose titanium windscreen/pot stand.

Awesome stoves: Trail Designs Keg-F system (I've used this for 5,000 miles), MSR Micro Rocket, Jetboil Flash or Flash Lite, Snow Peak GigaPower

Make your Own Super Lightweight Alcohol Stove for Free: Zenstoves.com

Water

As the number of hikers go up on the PCT, so does the chance for contamination of seemingly-clean water sources. In the desert, lots of PCT hikers make the poor and totally uncool choice to camp right next to water sources and bury their poop nearby. In addition, I've heard stories of a totally irresponsible PCT hiker washing her underwear right in the only natural water source for 30 miles! Plus, there's plenty of cattle grazing along portions of the trail. As a result, a bunch of the water on this trail is not nearly as clean as it looks (and plenty of sources are even dirtier than they look). What this means for you is you should purify all of your water or, at the very least, carry something that can deal with especially bad, clearly contaminated water.

I like using a filter because I can get clean water instantly. With chemicals, you have to wait 15 minutes to 4 hours. In the PCT desert, when I get to a water source, I'm usually thirsty enough that I don't have the patience to wait 15 minutes. That being said, chemicals are much lighter than filters and don't require maintenance. With the exception of bleach, however, chemicals are also more expensive over a thru-hike than many filters. When water resources are particularly... chunky... I pre-filter my water with a bandana, coffee filter, or fine mesh before running it through any filter or treatment system. That helps keep your filter from becoming prematurely clogged, as cleaning a clogged filter ranks pretty low on the scale of fun activities.

Every hiker is going to want to carry extra water capacity on the PCT. Most hikers leave the Mexico terminus with at least six liters of water. I usually carry at least two liters of extra water capacity than what I will regularly use for a section hike. This gives me flexibility to manage longer distances as needed or to carry extra water into a dry camp at night.

Awesome water filters/treatment (all of which I have used): Sawyer Squeeze, Aquamira, bleach drops, Polar Pure (for trips of 2 weeks or less)

Sun Protection

I know it looks weird carrying an umbrella on a sunny day, but the sun on the PCT—especially in the desert—can be unrelenting. I carry an umbrella to protect against the sun, rain, and wind. Look for a strong umbrella that will withstand a variety of weather conditions (definitely not the "Walmart Special," which will invert after one strong gust of wind). The PCT is such an exposed and sunny trail that many hikers opt for full-coverage long-sleeve sun shirts, long brimmed or skirted sunhats, and even sun gloves. And don't forget sunscreen and sunglasses—you'll definitely need them on this trail, as the "green tunnel effect" is far less common than on trails like the AT.

Awesome umbrellas: Montbell UL Trekking, Euroschirm (which also licenses to Gossamer Gear, Six Moon Designs, and Anti-Gravity Gear)

Bear Canisters

Backpackers are legally required to carry bear canisters through portions of the Sierra, most notably the stretch between Devil's Postpile and the northern Yosemite border. For PCT thru-hikers, it's easiest logistically to carry a bear can all the way from Kennedy Meadows to Sonora Pass;while this is a haul, this method is much better than having to get off the trail and back on just to grab a bear can every time you're about to enter a stretch that requires one. Bear cans weigh a minimum of around two pounds when empty, so prepare for some added weight. Before you go, check out a few models in person at REI to make sure you can open your chosen model easily (some of them are *extremely* hard for humans to open, not just those pesky bears). The National Park Service has a list of Sierra-approved bear canisters: bit.ly/pct-canisters. A few companies will allow you to rent the bear cans, which they will send to you at Kennedy Meadows. Check out http://www.wild-ideas.net/rental-faqs/ for more details.

Footwear

A hiker is nothing without properly-working feet, so choosing a good set of hiking shoes is essential. You'll be spending at least 8 hours on your feet every day, often over uneven terrain. Do them a solid and invest in some good gear.

Most PCT thru-hikers use mesh low-top trail-runners. These shoes dry more quickly than boots, which helps prevent overly-sweaty feet (and the blisters that moisture brings) in the desert. Mesh trail runners also dry more quickly after the numerous fords in the Sierra (most hikers ford with their hiking shoes on to allow for better stability).

Your hiking shoes should be comfortable, fit you well (won't bang your toes on the downhill), have solid tread, and have a firm-yet-flexible midsole. Most shoes come with a cardboard-thin insole, which may not be enough to support the constant pounding of a backpacker's gait. Thus, many hikers opt to pay extra for a separate footbed that supports their walking style much better than the provided insoles. To help extra sweat and moisture evaporate, take off your shoes and take out your footbeds during your breaks to let them dry out. This will help them last longer and prevent moisture-related rubbing inside your shoe.

To take care of your feet, you will also need to invest in quality socks. Many PCT thru-hikers prefer a light running sock or sock liner to prevent rubbing and overly sweaty feet. Having clean socks helps avoid the rubbing that can lead to blisters, so I always bring a couple of extra pairs.

A light gaiter is really useful on the PCT, where the trail is overrun with sand, dirt, and pine needles that can get in your shoes and cause foot rubbing and holes in your socks. Not all socks are equal, however; look for socks with a tight weave that will prevent dirt particles from getting to your feet, as they can cause rubbing and irritation. I like the Darn Tough ¼ Sock Light because they have a tight weave, are lightweight (1.2 oz per pair), and have a lifetime guarantee (the best of any gear in the industry). I like using Dirty Girl Gaiters due to the light weight, fun and colorful designs, and the versatility to work with almost any shoe.

Shoes are possibly a hiker's most personal piece of equipment. It may take you many models and a lot of foot pain on the trail to find the right shoe for you. Some brands run wider, some narrower; some have thicker sides, some are nearly paper-thin.. Some people can only hike in old school leather boots; some hike in feather-weight trail runners with little support. Whatever model you choose, know that, like a pregnant woman, your feet will grow and expand up to two full sizes over the course of your thru-hike. If you buy all your shoes before your hike and are having them sent to you, make sure to purchase a few pairs that are larger than your current size in preparation for the latter half of your hike.

Expect to get between 100-500 miles out of socks and between 300-600 miles out of shoes. One way to tell when shoes are "dead" is not just when they develop holes— though that's an obvious sign that it's time for some new footwear. Instead, look at the midsole, which is where the cushioning and support of your shoe is. If it looks compressed (squished, wrinkly, or "brain-like") and it isn't absorbing the blow of your footsteps, it is probably time to get new shoes. Another telltale sign that your shoes need replacement is if the outsole (the tread on your shoes) is as flat and bald as a used tire. Lastly, and most importantly, if you feel a body part starting to feel pain for no explicable reason (e.g., shin, back, hip, foot arch), it can often be remedied by switching your shoes. Plantar fasciitis is a *very* common ailment among thru-hikers, but it can be avoided by switching your shoes out often, using a supportive footbed, and performing daily foot stretches.

Shoes and socks don't last forever, so please do not call up companies complaining that your shoes didn't last all 2,650 miles. That kind of behavior makes all of us hikers look entitled, and it makes it harder for folks who have legitimate gear failures to be taken seriously. One of the few exceptions is Darn Tough socks, which offer a lifetime guarantee, even for thru-hikers.

Awesome shoes that are popular on the PCT: Altra Lone Peak or Olympus, Brooks Cascadia, Salomon Speedcross or X-Ultra, La Sportiva Mutants or Bushido

NOTE: Just because these shoes are popular doesn't necessarily mean that they will work for you. Make sure to thoroughly test your shoes before venturing off into the wilderness.

Clothing

To maximize versatility and temperature regulation, I subscribe to a layered clothing approach to thru-hiking. Each item is fairly minimal by itself (my insulated puffy jacket, for example, weighs only 8 ounces), but paired with other items, it can be as effective as a much heavier jacket. Below is the order of clothing I put on as temperatures go from hot to cold:

   Hot Temps (Base clothing): shorts and a sun shirt OR t-shirt OR tank-top > Windshirt > Long sleeve top and long john bottoms (tights) > Hat and gloves > Puffy jacket and wind pants > All my raingear (even when it isn't raining— raingear holds in the heat and keeps the out the wind)

   Coldest: Abandon hiking, set up my shelter, and get in my sleeping bag (seriously, don't risk hypothermia so you can get in "just a few more miles")

In the desert, many people opt for a long sleeve, light-colored, collared button-up shirt to maximize sun protection. Many find that lightweight, looser clothing is more comfortable and prevents sweaty fabric from sticking to your skin. If it's extremely hot during the peak of the day, many hikers find that hiking in a wet shirt or hat is a nice way to cool off (as long as you are confident it can dry before bedtime).

In the Sierra, expect to carry more warm clothing or heavy duty versions of clothes you carried earlier in the trail. In Northern California, you can often switch to a setup that's similar to the one you might have in the desert (it is often toasty during prime thru-hiker season). In Oregon—and especially in Washington—be prepared for cooler temps, rain, and possibly even snow; this is a good time to implement quick-drying and synthetic insulating layers.

If you're looking to save a few bucks on gear, clothing is a spot where the cheapo-brand option won't kill you. A lot of hikers have been happy with thrift store finds or Target-brand clothes. Frog Toggs is a popular lightweight $20 raingear used by many thru-hikers. Look for synthetic fabrics, merino wool, or a blend of these materials for all your layers except your puffy layer. If you're keeping your pack weight down, stay away from a lot of spandex—it's heavier and doesn't dry as quickly). There are some downsides to using discount clothing, however: they are often less durable than larger "name brand" athletic gear, and they typically smell worse when you are sweaty. Still, the savings you make by going cheap on clothes may be worth a few wrinkled noses from fellow hikers.

While cheapo-brand base layers and midlayers may work well for your needs, a puffy (insulated) jacket is one piece of clothing worth investing in. A good down jacket is like a good down sleeping bag: it can last for decades and will be among your last lines of defense against hypothermia. Pay close attention to the fill of a puffy jacket: synthetic insulation stays warm when wet, whereas down does not, so some hikers opt to carry a synthetic puffy jacket. Also, even a good synthetic jacket will cost significantly less than a lower quality down jacket. And of course, higher quality insulated layers will typically keep you warmer. If you can, test out your puffy before you're stuck in the woods in wet, freezing temperatures.

Puffy Jacket Recommendations: Montbell Thermawrap, Montbell UL Parka, Western Mountaineering Flash Jacket, Mountain Hardware Ghost Whisperer, Uniqlo Ultralight Down Jacket (at $70, this fashion brand actually makes a decent down)

Snow gear

During most years, snow lingers on high passes in the Sierra and especially on Mt. Whitney (southbounders should expect snow in Washington as well). Crossing snow may require special gear, but first, let me explain how PCT hikers find themselves crossing steep and icy snowfields.

The PCT is designed to stay close to the crest of several mountain ranges. As a result, you will go up and over passes (the low spot between two mountains) to get from one basin to another on your way to Canada. To get to those passes, you will typically take the nicely graded and switch-backed PCT (which has an approximate 10% grade) as it ascends a much steeper (possibly 40 degree) slope. However, when the trail and that slope are covered in snow—and you can't see the trail at all—you will still need to get up and over that 40 degree slope, only now without the guidance of the PCT. So now, to follow the PCT's general path, you will need to traverse what is essentially a steep ski slope in order to reach the pass and journey on toward the next basin.

That means you're going to have to climb some mountains in the snow. Time to get your adventure on.

Many PCT hikers opt to tackle this feat with the aid of an ice axe. However, if you decide to carry an ice axe, learn ahead of time how to self-arrest and take it off of your pack when you cross snow in steeper places. I've heard way too many stories from Search & Rescue crews about people who have died from slips on snow and ice whose ice axes were still strapped to their pack instead of gripped in their hands. An ice axe can be useless—or even worse, dangerous—if you don't know how to use it properly. Before you go, take a class on how to self-arrest and watch instructional YouTube videos. At the very least, during a lunch break on the PCT, practice in non-scary snow conditions with more experienced hikers.

To aid in crossing icy slopes in the morning, some hikers opt to use Kahtoohla Microspikes or Yaktrax. Both of these items are like crampons, but they can be worn with trail runners, are significantly lighter, and require less skill and training to use than crampons. Subsequently, these are less aggressive than traditional crampons, but most PCT thru-hikers find that they are sufficient for typical early-summer PCT conditions (note that while traction devices are useful for crossing icy slopes in the morning, they aren't much help after the snow softens up in the afternoon; be sure to plan ahead if you are expecting snowy/icy conditions). You can also use sheet metal screws to create make-shift crampons with your trail runners (check YouTube for directions). Springtime snow conditions in the Sierra aren't quite suited to snowshoes, so most thru-hikers do not carry them—they usually end up being extra, useless weight.

Some hikers opt to just use their hiking poles through snowy areas. If this is your choice, then you may want to opt for a heavier, sturdier pole (i.e. not carbon fiber).

When traveling on snow, don't forget to wear plenty of sunscreen (to prevent sunburns) and sunglasses (to prevent snow blindness). Snow has a nasty tendency to bounce sunlight off of the ground and back at your face at angles you might not think about initially; thus, when you apply sunscreen, apply it not only to the usual spots, but also to weird places like the bottom of your chin, ears, nostrils, under your forearms, and back of knees.

For northbound PCT hikers, your feet will often be cold and wet in the Sierra. Some hikers like to wear waterproof socks over their normal socks to prevent their feet from going numb. I also wear an eVent calf or knee-high gaiter to keep snow out of my shoe. If it gets below freezing at night, bring your wet gear inside your tent and put it inside of a waterproof bag (like your pack liner), and then place the bag/liner inside your empty backpack to prevent everything from freezing solid the next morning.

Navigation

Every PCT thru-hiker should include navigational gear as an essential part of their pack weight. Although the PCT is generally well-marked, snow can make the trail virtually invisible for miles. That's right: you could walk on snow as far as you can see with the trail being "somewhere" underneath 5 feet of opaque white stuff.

Most hikers carry a PCT app with them on their phone. However, don't let your phone app be your only navigational tool: batteries die, phones get wet, screens crack, hikers die. Halfmile puts out *free* maps that you can print yourself found at: https://www.pctmap.net/maps/. Just be sure to have a basic understanding of map-reading skills—you don't have to be an expert, but being able to keep track of your position will help you anticipate upcoming sections and develop your orienteering skills. The PCT is one trail where reading a map and knowing how to use a compass are a huge plus, particularly when Mother Nature decides to make things difficult.

Unlike the AT, trail intersections aren't always marked on the PCT. *If you step over a long stick that is covering the trail, it's often there to indicate that you have stepped onto a trail that isn't the PCT.* Hikers who come before you will sometimes draw arrows in the dirt at intersections to help guide the way. Refrain from the temptation of taking your Sharpie to trail signs, however, as this violates Leave No Trace principles. Navigation, while sometimes a pain, is also part of the intellectual fun of the PCT. You didn't decide to do this because it was easy, did you?

Electronics

These days, almost everyone carries a smartphone on the PCT. While it's poor trail etiquette to chat or text while you're walking on the trail, phones can be a good way to stay in touch with folks at home when you're in town or at camp.

If you're carrying a phone, consider how you're going to charge it during the long haul between resupplies. Some hikers opt for a solar panel or extra external battery to charge their phone during the long haul between resupplies. Also, it is highly worth investing in a good waterproof and dust-proof phone case.

Some hikers carry additional electronics like MP3 players, Kindles, and even iPads. You'll likely want photos of the PCT better than what your phone can capture, so consider bringing a good point-and-shoot, mirrorless, or even a DSLR camera.

Expect your electronics to take up a minimum of an extra half pound in your pack. Before you go, label all your electronics with a Sharpie or paint pen in case you leave your phone charging at a restaurant or drop your camera at the top of Mt. Whitney. That may just be enough to fix what might have been a very expensive mistake.

Gear Use and Care

The PCT is not a gentle trail for any piece of gear. There are plenty of spiky plants, rough rocks, and wildlife eager to chew on your gear. Here are a few tips to make your gear last for the whole trail.

1. Before you go, pre-treat your clothing and gear with Permethrin to repel mosquitoes and ticks. Although Lyme disease is rare along the PCT, there have been reported cases here and there, and mosquito clouds on the PCT can sometimes rival the ones seen in tropical countries.
2. Dry your sleeping bag and shelter out every day. When you take your lunch break, take out your sleeping bag and let the condensation evaporate. Even if you don't think your gear got wet, this process will help restore the loft to your bag and prevent mold build-up.
3. Keep your zippers clean. The sand and near-invisible silt on the PCT make zippers especially prone to failure. Lube up your zippers with a product like like ZipCare before you go, and expect to give them another cleaning half-way up the trail.
4. Bring your shoes, hiking poles, and pack into your shelter at night. The wildlife loves to gnaw on the gear that has absorbed the salt from your sweat..
5. Wash your gear at least once on your thru-hike and again immediately afterwards. Salt and dirt can slowly abrade your gear. Oil and dirt work their way into the down in your sleeping bag, making it less

lofty. Washing takes the smell out of your clothes and makes you more appealing to trail angels and potential trail dates. Use soap that is appropriate for your gear—tech washes for backpacks and down wash for any down sleeping bag or down clothing (McNett or NikWax sell both types). Thru-hikers are renegades, but be sure to *actually follow the directions* on the bottle when you wash your gear. Otherwise, you might find yourself replacing hundreds of dollars' worth of gear.

6. Whenever you set your gear down, look where you are placing it first. This prevents you from setting your pack on a cactus, some rough rocks, or heck, even a rattlesnake!

7. Always carry your pack by the haul loop on top or by the pack straps. I've seen packs rip from being carried by the body fabric.

8. Carry repair kits, a needle and thread, and repair tape (or duct tape) and know how to use them correctly.

Last Thoughts on Gear

The best gear is not necessarily the lightest: it's the gear that makes you feel safe and comfortable and happy, over the long haul of your hike, given your skill level, experience, and knowledge. The gear we carry helps alleviate our fears, whether they be fears of cold, rain, loneliness, or boredom. All gear choices are a balance, and only *you* know what is going to work best for you.

You'll hear a lot of talk about non-essential gear as being "luxury items," as if that's a bad thing. The thing about luxury items is that they *do* serve a purpose. That purpose is making you feel psychologically safe and happy. I once watched a shakedown where an ultralight gear critic told a devout Christian that his Bible wasn't an essential part of his pack. I've hiked thousands of miles with two stuffed turtles weighing 10.4 oz total. But those turtles, just like that Bible did for my fellow hiker, serve a distinct purpose to the person carrying them.

Whatever gear you choose, make sure that each item is serving its purpose and not just sitting at the bottom of your pack. *You should be using all the gear you carry almost every day you are on trail.* As a rule of thumb, if I've gone a week on trail without using something, I'll send it home or mail it up trail to a place I think I might need it (a few items, like raingear, parts of my med kit, and shelter stay with me regardless). I used those turtles as pillows and to cheer me up, and my buddy read his Bible every night before bed (admittedly, he could've used a Kindle app on his phone, but maybe it wouldn't have meant the same to him).

Picking your gear can seem intimidating, but the more you know, the better your chances of feeling safe and comfortable in your gear and on the trail. No matter what gear you end up using for the PCT, how heavy or light it is, or how cheap or expensive it may be, practice packing and setting up your camp system in your yard, at a car camping site, and on overnight backpacking trips. Do this long before you leave for the PCT, and make sure to practice in rain, wind, snow and other less-than-ideal conditions. Testing your equipment beforehand has other perks: should you not feel safe or comfortable, you can bail back to your car and go home. And it is a heck of a lot easier to return or resell an unwanted piece of gear when you're at home compared to from the PCT. By being familiar and comfortable with your gear before you start the trail, you will have already taken one of the most important steps on the entire PCT.

Disclosure of gear affiliations:

On a long distance backpacking trip, I don't compromise my safety or comfort by using bad gear for any reason— even if it is free. I only work with companies whose products I've seriously tested and love enough to recommend to my friends and strangers. These companies include: Gossamer Gear, Mountain Laurel Designs, Altra, Darn Tough Socks, Montbell, Sawyer, Trail Designs, Purple Rain Skirts, ProBar, and Alpine Aire. These companies, in my opinion, offer the best gear for my thru-hiking needs, which is why they are among the gear items I mention in this chapter. I also suggest gear from companies that are not my sponsors that I've also found to work well, or are otherwise popular on the PCT.

A Word from the PCTA

L ong distance backpacking has had a profoundly positive impact on my life. Getting lost in the backcountry is my peace, my wisdom, my reset button, my church. To keep this a secret would be selfish, and it is for these reasons that I enthusiastically encourage *everyone* to head out onto the trail. If we all found time to connect with nature, I have no doubt this would be a better, happier, more conscientious planet.

That said, growing foot traffic on the trails isn't without negative consequence. This is especially true for those who discover backpacking prior to learning the importance of trail etiquette and conservation. For this reason, I strongly encourage everyone who reads this book to learn and practice the principles of Leave No Trace, found at https://lnt.org/learn/7-principles.

Additionally, in order to protect our trails' future, it's essential that we lend support to the organizations who preserve and oversee these national treasures. In the case of the Pacific Crest Trail, this means giving our support to Pacific Crest Trail Association. Because Carly and I want future generations to have the same opportunity to experience the PCT's pristine beauty, five percent of the proceeds from your purchase of this book go to the PCTA.

But why stop there?

We've asked our friends at the PCTA to share a few words on other ways you can support the Pacific Crest Trail.

Tattooed on your soul.

You are the Pacific Crest Trail.

Zach and Carly have done a wonderful job sharing their insights about traveling on the PCT. On your journey, you will also discover what it is about this special trail that drives the rest of us to be so crazy passionate about it. And once you find it, we promise it never will leave you.

The PCT is life changing. Friends. Communities. Landscapes. This idea that a 2,650-mile trail across stunning mountain ranges can exist.

You're the future of the PCT. Without passionate people like you this trail never would have been built and couldn't exist today. The PCT needs you. Shout out about how incredible it is. Step up and support it.

You are the Pacific Crest Trail Association. Join the cause. Donate. Volunteer. Together, we're going to preserve this incredible wilderness experience for younger generations to follow in our footsteps.

You can help protect this national treasure by joining the PCTA.

Your $35 annual membership will ensure that this trail and the experiences it provides will never end. Contact us and make a donation today.

1331 Garden Highway
Sacramento, CA 95833
(916) 285-1846
www.pcta.org - info@pcta.org

PACIFIC CREST TRAIL

ASSOCIATION

Appendices

Liz Thomas' Gear Checklist

Big Four

- ☐ Backpack
- ☐ Pack Liner
- ☐ Sleeping Pad
- ☐ Shelter
- ☐ Shelter Poles
- ☐ Stakes
- ☐ Guylines (may be attached to shelter)
- ☐ Sleeping bag or quilt
- ☐ Groundsheet or bivy sack

Clothing (both worn and carried)

- ☐ Underwear (one to wear; you may opt for extra)
- ☐ Baselayer (t-shirt, tank-top, or long sleeve sunshirt)
- ☐ Long sleeve baselayer for warmth and wicking
- ☐ Long john bottoms
- ☐ Puffy jacket (insulating layer)
- ☐ Raingear jacket or poncho
- ☐ Raingear bottom (skirt/kilt or pants; some PCT hikers go without)
- ☐ Windshirt
- ☐ Warm thin gloves
- ☐ Sun hat
- ☐ Sunglasses
- ☐ Neck Protection (bandana)
- ☐ Cold hat (beanie or balaklava)
- ☐ Watch (easier to check the time than your phone)
- ☐ Sleep clothes (some people just sleep in their hiking clothes)
- ☐ Clothing stuff sack

Footwear

- [ ] Socks (one to wear; you may opt for extra)
- [ ] Lightweight gaiters (some PCT hikers go without)
- [ ] Shoes
- [ ] Insoles/Footbeds

Cooking and Hydration

- [ ] Stove
- [ ] Windscreen
- [ ] Fuel bottle (if going with a liquid fuel—mark your bottle FUEL so you don't accidentally mistake it for water)
- [ ] Fuel
- [ ] Matches/lighter
- [ ] Cook pot
- [ ] Cook pot lid
- [ ] Utensils
- [ ] Cook kit storage bag
- [ ] Bear protection (canister, hang system, Odor Proof Sack, or a combo)
- [ ] Water storage
- [ ] Spare water storage
- [ ] Water treatment

Random Small Items

- [ ] Headlamp or flashlight
- [ ] Whistle (may be on your backpack's sternum strap)
- [ ] Blade or knife (some hikers don't carry this)
- [ ] Trekking poles (some hikers don't carry this—but if your shelter requires it, you should)
- [ ] Bug headnet (may be useful for parts of Sierra, Oregon, and/or Washington)
- [ ] Reading glasses (if you need them)
- [ ] Repair items (needle/thread, safety pin, duct tape)
- [ ] Compass
- [ ] Maps
- [ ] Guidebook pages or Town guide pages
- [ ] PCT Water Report (For the desert)

☐ Wallet with your PCT permit, cash, ID, ATM card, credit card, health care info, and important phone #s

☐ Your passport and Get Into Canada Free Visa (only just before you get into Canada)

☐ Phone

☐ Phone charger

☐ External battery and/or solar charger

☐ Camera and SD card with the oh-so-optional Stickpic or Gorilla Pod (for selfies)

☐ Other electronics (mp3 player or kindle)

☐ Potty trowel

☐ Journal and pen (waterproof paper is nice here)

☐ Bag to carry these items

☐ Hairbands

☐ Umbrella

Hygiene and Health

☐ Sunscreen

☐ Bug spray (may be useful for parts of Sierra, Oregon, and/or Washington)

☐ Toothbrusth

☐ Toothpaste

☐ Biodegradeable soap in a small dropper (some hikers don't bring this)

☐ Toilet paper (some hikers don't bring this)

☐ Contact lens/solution

☐ A bag to put this all in (can be a ziplock bag or you may keep it in your hipbelt pockets)

Med Kit

☐ Blister care

☐ Sports tape

☐ Triple antibiotic in small single-serving packet

☐ Band-Aids (just a few)

☐ Hydrocortisone (in a small single serving packet)

☐ Anti-diarrhea pills

☐ Gas X

- ☐ Anti-heart burn pills
- ☐ Benadryl
- ☐ Tylenol PM
- ☐ Pain killers (ibuprofen, naproxen, etc.)
- ☐ Excedrin
- ☐ Alcohol prep pad
- ☐ Hand sanitzer
- ☐ Krazy glue mini
- ☐ Prescription meds

It's really cold and/or you're in the snow

- ☐ Puffy bottoms (insulating layer—may be a nice addition for the Sierra or if it is cold in Washington)
- ☐ Waterproof glove or mitt shells (may be a nice addition for the Sierra or if it's cold in Washington)
- ☐ Windpants
- ☐ Synthetic puffy layer
- ☐ Microspikes
- ☐ Ice axe
- ☐ Waterproof socks (your feet will often be wet for most of the Sierra)

I am thru-hiking the Pacific Crest Trail because...

When I successfully thru-hike the Pacific Crest Trail, I will...

If I give up on the Pacific Crest Trail, I will...

CONNECT WITH THE AUTHORS

Zach Davis

URL: appalachiantrials.com/author/zach
Facebook: facebook.com/theGoodBadger
Twitter: @zrdavis
Instagram: @zrdavis
Email: theGoodBadger@gmail.com

Carly Moree

Instagram: @carly.moree
Email: carly.moree@gmail.com